THE 7 LAWS OF LOVE

How To Live a Life of Value, Purpose, and True Success

Jim Hetherington

The 7 Laws of Love
How to Live a Life of Value, Purpose, and True Success
Jim Hetherington
www.JimHetherington.com

Copyright © 2019 by Jim Hetherington

ISBN: 978-1-77277-311-8

No part of this publication may be reproduced, stored in a retrieval system or transmitted in any form or by any means, electronic, mechanical, photocopying, recording, scanning or otherwise. Limit of Liability/Disclaimer of Warranty: While the author has used her best effort in preparing this book, she makes no representations or warranties with respect to the accuracy or completeness of the content of this book and specifically disclaim any implied warranties of merchantability or fitness for a particular group. The author is not providing medical advice and are not writing anything against the medical and pharmaceutical industry. No warranty may be created or extended by sales representatives or written sales materials. The advice and strategies contained herein may not be suitable for your situation. You should consult with a professional where appropriate. Neither the publisher nor author shall be liable for any loss of profit or any other commercial damages, including but not limited to special, incidental, consequential, or other damages. Readers should be aware that Internet Websites offered as citations and/or sources for further information may have changed or disappeared between the time this was written and when it is read. All rights reserved, including the right to reproduce this book or portions thereof in any form whatsoever.

Published by:
10-10-10 Publishing
Markham, Ontario

Contents

Dedication	vii
Reviews About Jim Hetherington and His Work	ix
A Letter from Jim	xi

Part 1 – In the Beginning	**1**
Purpose	2
Magnify Your Effect on Others	7
Set Apart	10
Can't Fight the Laws	11
3 Keys	12

Part 2 – Time	**17**
Can't Fight Time and Change	17
Potential Must Change to Ability	18
T = Take Control	20
I = Implement New Patterns	22
M = Make ME a Priority	24
E = Execute Daily	27
Schedule Your Time	27
All You Get is 168	29
Try Not to Change	30

Part 3 – Attitude   **37**
It's Everything   39
A is for Adjust   43
T is for Think   44
T is for Talk   46
I is for Invest   47
This T is for Trust   49
U is for Undo   51
D is for Determine   52
E is for Example   54

Part 4 – Heart to Heart   **59**
Look in the Mirror   59
Values   63
Purpose   66
Success   67
Beliefs That May be Keeping You From Success   68
Preparation is the Key to Lasting Success   71

Part 5 – Balance   **75**
Physical World   76
Relational World   76
Business and Career World   76
Spiritual World   76
Keep the Pressure Equal   80
My Caution   83
It's Crucial to Keep Balance   84
Your Future

Part 6 – The Laws of Love — 91
7 Types of Love — 92
7 Laws of Love — 97
7 Lies of Love — 109
7 Things Love Hates — 119
7 Layers of Love — 123

Part 7 – Success Principles — 131
Define Your Success — 131
Values-Purpose-Success — 132
Structures — 135
Systems — 136
Strategies — 138
Speech — 140
Sacrifice — 142
Sustain — 146
Seize — 148
Stop — 151
Start — 152
Smile — 154

Part 8 – What Now? — 161
Red Lights Are Good — 161
What Are You Waiting For? — 165
Make a Plan — 167
Next Steps for You! — 169

About the Author — 175

Dedication

While writing this book, I became aware of the number of people who have shaped my thinking which has shaped me as a man. I'm grateful for the people who share their wisdom and knowledge from when I was young until now. Recently people like T.D. Jakes, Brian Tracy, Les Brown and Tony Robbins are some of the big names that have influenced my thinking as I have read and studied under them. As well as my close coaches, mentors and friends like Jeffrey Krugg, James MacNeil and Raymond Aaron have had a major hand in my life as I've crafted this book, so thank you all.

My amazing wife Mary continues to be a strong support and source of encouragement to me; I wouldn't be where I am without her.

Most importantly I'm thankful for the unending source of love and wisdom I receive daily from God, without which I would be empty.

Reviews About Jim Hetherington and His Work

We worked alongside Jim for a number of years when he was a youth leader. We watched him become a father figure to hurting youth who had "father issues" and he loved them back to life.

We are grateful to have been impacted by Jim and witness his commitment over the years to teach and instruct people, and we're confident in his ability to share insights and truths that will help people grow.
- Tony and Rhonda Davison

We had such a great day and you played such a big part in that for us. We absolutely loved our wedding ceremony and the way you delivered it. You were professional and calming, while also making the mood light for us. We appreciate the work you did leading up to the ceremony and meeting with us to ensure we had a great ceremony. Truly, thank you so much.
- Alison and Justin Vasey

We are so thankful for Jim; he is the definition of a mentor and a coach. He is so professional and listens without judgement. We are so thankful for someone like him to give us encouragement and the tools for all relationships.
- Sarah and Brandon Lovegrove

The 7 Laws of Love is an incredible resource, not only for couples but for entrepreneurs as well. This book will enhance every relationship that you experience in your life, including the teller at the bank, the clerk at the checkout as well as all of your acquaintances and business partners alike. Jim Hetherington's TIME and ATTITUDE formulas are fabulous tools that you can easily incorporate into your day and life experiences. I highly recommend this latest release by Jim as it is a priceless guide. Not only will all of your relationships benefit, but you will experience insights into success mindsets which are critical for all entrepreneurs as well.
- Dr. Stacey Cooper

Jim Hetherington nails it with these seven steps! He is a brilliant author who is able to define steps that you can easily implement to a better you, to the delight of everyone around you. Jim is honest and passionate about your true success. This book is a must read!
- Jeff Ramsperger

Our life is about relationships. Jim's coaching has made me more aware of not only my relationship with myself but how I interact with others. He has made wise suggestions for improving my relationship with others, particularly in being more effective in my dating.
- Larry Cooper

A Letter from Jim

"If love is the answer, what is the question?"
– Jim Hetherington

From the beginning of time, love was woven into the fabric the world. Love existed before you or I ever came to be. The problem is that love has been misrepresented, miscommunicated, and misinterpreted for centuries.

Wars and disputes have been fought in the name of love and God. Philosophers and teachers have given us their understanding of love. And of course, life experience has sometimes tainted our view on love.

With the passing of time and the experiences we come into, barriers are put up between us and the true understanding of love. If we are rejected by a parent, a barrier goes up. If a friend offends us, a barrier goes up. If we are hurt in a romantic relationship, a barrier goes up. Over time, it becomes increasingly difficult to see love clearly.

Even in our day-to-day interactions with work colleagues or clients, barriers can be put up, making it more challenging to communicate. Getting cut off in traffic, or being misunderstood when we try to do something kind for a stranger... these can all put up barriers, and keep us from experiencing love at its fullest.

Love is at the center of everything that we do. Love is the driving force, being at the center of every act of kindness and generosity. It's the driving force behind caring, consideration, and compassion. And the further we are removed from seeing its true form, the more challenging life becomes.

The only way to get back to experiencing the fullest that life has to give, is to see love for its truest form. And the only way we can do that is to remove the barriers. Barriers are removed when we examine our hearts and begin to make correct choices to express love in its fullest.

Journey with me through this book, and you will begin to see strategies to begin to remove the barriers. You and I need to have a clear view of love so that we can walk out in the fullest experience of love, and share that with the world. The world needs to see love expressed in every relationship. Our homes need to experience more love. Our family, friends, and business associates need to experience more love.

Change will only happen by you first reflecting love to others, not insisting that others love you first.
– Jim Hetherington

By this I mean that true love must be a reflection of your heart first. You can't expect others to automatically love you just because you want them to. There needs to be something lovable in you that attracts them to you in the first place. You may get some that are close to you, like family, to love you regardless of your disposition, but even that will wear off after a while. You need to reflect love.

How can we do this?

As Tony Robins says, you have to change yourself first.

You want to change the world, start with yourself first. You can't change anyone else but you. But you may say, "My husband really needs to change his attitude." You may be right, but you can't force your husband to do anything—you can only change yourself first. "But you don't understand, Jim. My boss is a total jerk." I get it, but until we work on everything that we possibly can in our own lives first, there is nothing we can do to change anyone else. When they see change in us, then maybe. Or we may find that as we change, we will begin to see that the other things don't bother us nearly as much.

Through this journey, we will look at ourselves more deeply. We will examine our attitude, and discover that a good mental attitude is key to health and success. We will look at success principles, and time and purpose, and leading a balanced life. Plus, we'll examine the laws and lies of love, as well as the layers of love, and the things love hates, and so much more.

Grab a journal book, or use the blank pages in the book for you and take good notes. Don't be afraid to reach out to me as well. I'm available on my website, at jimhetherington.com, or if you want to get in touch with me by email, you can contact me at jim@jimhetherington.com. You can also connect with me on social media. Go to www.coachjim360.com to get all my contact info.

If you have your pen and paper ready, let's get started.

Part 1

In the Beginning

"Change yourself first, and you may find that others don't look so bad."
– Jim Hetherington

It's been said that you can't have it all. But I think that's wrong.

You can have it all. By that, I mean that you can enjoy successful and fulfilled relationships, meaningful and powerful friendships, and a great and rewarding career.

Wouldn't that be amazing! Imagine right now, if you will, what that would look like. What would a perfect, balanced life look like for you? What does a perfect world of relationships look like for you?

Sit where you are for a moment more, and consider this. How would it change your life? What do you need to change in order to achieve this? What would it feel like for you to have the relationships you want?

Take a few minutes before you continue and journal some thoughts of what a perfect home life would look like. What about relationships with a spouse or partner, children or grandchildren? How about work or business, what would the ideal work environment look like? How about friends? Your spiritual life, what would that look like? Pause and write your thoughts now so you can reflect as you journey through the book.

There are ways to build successful businesses and corporations, and not be lonely when you get to the top of the success mountain. There are ways to have your personal success story come true, and be surrounded by people you love and adore, and that love and adore you back.

Once you have defined your success, what it will look like, and how you will know you've achieved it, you can be wonderfully happy.

Take a walk through these pages with me, and begin the journey to wonderful success and magnificent relationships along the way. Also, take the challenge and redefine the existence you are experiencing now, and shape it into a joy-filled reality. You can rewrite the script and have the satisfying life you have always wanted.

Purpose

Many good coaches, mentors, or teachers challenge their clients or students to find their *why*.

As a coach, I work with people to discover their purpose, then the why answers itself.

Many people try to find their purpose in their possessions. Others try to find it in their career or job. Others just try to find it in other people; they live vicariously through others. Some just never really truly discover their purpose, and settle for living out other people's, with them or for them. For many, they rely on others to *complete them* or *make them happy*. Take it from me, if someone says to you that you complete them or that you make them happy, RUN—as quickly as you can! You are not responsible for making someone complete or happy. And you don't want to get into a relationship with someone who is incomplete or unhappy—do you?

You want to be in a relationship with a person that understands who they are. You want to enter into a relationship with someone that is complete in who they are, and who will take responsibility for their own mood (happiness). That's complete. Love is complete when two people that know their full purpose and life direction join together to build a future, not when one hitches themselves to another in order for that person to make them whole.

If you already know where you are going and who you are, you don't need someone who is unsure about themselves and their future, hitching themselves to you in order that they "feel" complete. That should never be your life ambition.

A love relationship is not a 50%-50% deal. It's a 100%-100% deal. Both sides put in 100% all the time. You don't want to be connecting with someone that can only contribute 50% of their heart, ambition and desire to the relationship. You don't want to be in a relationship where the other person is trying to figure it out. NO! Get in a relationship from the start with someone that has a strong idea of who they are and where they are going. If they don't know where they are going, how do you know they are heading in the right direction for you?

One of the biggest problems in marriage is the commitment from partners from the beginning. The relationship can't start with one having one foot in and the other one outside uncommitted. When two people enter into marriage if they are not both in 100% it will present problems. You can't play half in and half out, it's ALL in.

The same holds true for any relationship, business or

personal; all parties need to be equally committed to the success.

It's important that you seek out a person who is as complete and as whole as one can be. If you have to start mending and patching someone to help them keep it together or find themselves… well, you really need to be looking somewhere else.

Does this make sense?

Life is too short, and time is too valuable. The last thing you need is to get involved with someone that is incomplete and is counting on someone else to complete them.

In no way am I talking about being perfect. I mean, none of us will ever be perfect. However, you need to know what your values are, what you stand for, and where your life is going, and then find someone that has at least done the same ground work. They, too, will know what they value. They will understand their purpose, and the direction of their life will line up with yours. If they line up, you are at least starting on the right foot.

Before getting into a relationship, I encourage you to look at what your core values are. This will help you to know who you are, and then you can begin to look for people that line up with your values. In my book, *Your Relationship Rescue Handbook*, I examine eleven areas of life, and challenge people to understand what they value in these areas. Once you know your values, it makes it easier to know who you are looking for because you will be looking for someone who shares the same values.

I strongly suggest writing out a Value Statement as part of your journey through this book. What are the things that you stand for? What are your core values? Look at the things that you will not compromise. Not in your life or with the one whom you want to share your life with.

If you want to learn more, and to receive more direction in

this key area, reach out to me at jim@jimhetherington.com, or go to my website, www.jimhetherington.com, and learn more about my book and this valuable tool.

It's the same with partnerships in business too. You want to get into businesses or work for companies that have an understanding of who they are and what they are doing. When you join forces with them, you are simply adding your gifts and talents to increase the performance and the power of the company.

You want to be involved with companies that have clear and defined purpose and mission statements. They should have a good vision, and a great values statement as well. If they don't, reconsider. If you're being hired for a position where you are building a team or restructuring part of the company, then great. But if you are running a company yourself, without any of these things in place, then we need to talk. Or if you are considering joining forces with a company that has none of these things in place we need to talk.

Seriously!

Reach out to me at jim@jimhetherington.com, and we can get together immediately to get to work on building these crucial pieces for your business. You can't expect people to follow a company that has no clear understanding of why they exist and what they are really all about.

There are many people in companies that will try. They will try to influence you to adopt their purpose, even though they are not clear on it themselves. Companies do this all the time. They try to convince people to sign up to sell their products or promote their business with the intent of just making money. The owners or managers have no interest in the company. The only interest that they have is to sell and to make money. They don't care about values, vision, or purpose.

Some people will go along with the selling of products, or making products that they don't really care about, because they've been convinced that by doing so, it will make them more complete or satisfied. Or, the company sells them on an image that they can obtain by doing so. You will soon become dissatisfied believing it will make you happy, rather than being complete as a person before you begin.

What happens is that the owner or manager is not really into it. The person or employee isn't really into it. They only exist to make money and pay their bills, and that's all.

Then what happens is a growing unsettling feeling that just can't be shaken. And there are people working endless hours in jobs they just don't like, all over the place, all the time. All the while, they are just thinking about being on the outside. They spend their time daydreaming, wishing for something better.

Let me ask you again. What are your values? What is your purpose? Where is your future taking you?

Money and success don't make you a better person. You need to be content with who you are as a person, with or without money. You need to define yourself as a person.

I think all of us would agree that there are basic things that we want in life. We want to be surrounded by people that we love and that love us. We want to do something that we enjoy, that brings meaning and satisfaction; we want to make good money at it, and we want to enjoy a happy life. That, in essence, sums up what most of us want—to live life on our terms.

The trick is, how do we get there? How do we have the relationships that we want? How do we find ourselves in the careers that we desire? How do we become successful?

The big question is, can we really have all this?

The answer is yes!

To get there, there are some fundamental shifts that we

need to make in our thinking. We need to adjust our mindsets.

Most people go through school to study a particular area, and then graduate in that area and get a job. That's the normal approach to making a living. The problem is, sometimes the things that we do academically are not the things that we are really gifted to do.

I recall one teacher that my son had in high school. This person was clearly very intelligent and very articulate, and they really knew the subject well. However, they were not a teacher. They had no skill whatsoever in communicating their knowledge to the students in a way that they could understand it. They simply opened the book and tried to shovel the material into the student's mind. They talk to people from their knowledge, in a way that says that you should know this, because I know it. This is knowledge-based teaching and not passion-based teaching. The latter is the kind of teaching that goes from the teacher's heart to the students, and into their minds; the former is from the head, and doesn't hit the heart at all.

Just because a person gets a degree in a particular area, doesn't mean that that's what their life purpose is. But isn't that exactly what we all want—to discover our life's purpose; to do the very thing that we were put on this planet to do; to do the thing that we are really gifted at?

People have spent countless hours looking for why they exist—looking to find the meaning of life and the very purpose that they're here. The problem is that they look in every place except in the one place where they will find it: on the inside.

Magnify Your Effect on Others

I believe that each of us has been put on this planet for a reason. Inside each one of us are seeds: seeds of potential, seeds of greatness, seeds of creativity, and seeds of achievement. The reality is that few of us really examine what it is that we are good at, and then pursue it. Many of us will take aptitude tests to try to find out what we are best suited to do. The problem is, the only thing this usually shows the person is how they can apply those gifts to professions that already exist. They take a person's aptitude, and manipulate the results to fit careers for which there are degree programs already.

Now, this test may help some people to get going in the right direction; however, I believe that a person needs to look on the inside. If you took a piece of fruit and opened it up, you would find the seeds of that fruit inside. The purpose of those seeds is to reproduce that fruit. Those seeds in the fruit are what they should be. An apple can't be a pear. As hard as it might want to be a pear, it cannot be one. It's the same with us.

There are seeds in us, and when those seeds are put in the right environment, with the right nutrients, they will grow and succeed in producing our purpose. That is our gift.

You and I need to look at the thing that we're gifted to do, and then pursue that and do it. Do the thing that is most natural to you. If you love to serve, then find ways that you can serve. If you like building things, then find ways that you can build things. Find the area that you are gifted in, pursue it, and you will begin to grow toward the area that will bring a successful and rewarding life for you.

In order for us to be successful, and to really achieve the goal of doing the thing that we are really gifted at, we need to adjust our way of thinking. For many of us, we look at others as being leaders, and we follow them. I believe that we are all called to be leaders. That doesn't mean that we don't listen to others around us, and just go around giving direction to ourselves. We do need to have structure and order. At the same time, we all need to take responsibility and actively pursue our dreams and passions. We need to start taking responsibility for ourselves and the others around us. Don't wait for others to show you what you should do. Begin to take initiative for your own life by exercising your gifts and growing them. All the while, you will encourage others around you to do the same.

An amazing thing will begin to happen. As you begin to grow and mature, other people in your circle will begin to grow and mature as well. You will all become your very best. This is the amazing process of influence. When you become your best, you become an influence to others around you. Then it continues on and on.

This can happen in any area of life: in our personal and family life, our romantic life, and our business life, and even our spiritual life.

Whether we want to be a leader in our own company, a leader in our home, or a leader in a local community group, there are a few simple things that we need to recognize.

The first is attitude. We need to have a good mental position. We need to constantly challenge how we think, and examine why we think the way we do. We need to continually examine our own hearts and check to see if there's anything that we need to correct.

We're going to examine attitude deeper, in a later chapter; but for now, I want to lay the groundwork for what we need to do as a leader.

Next is attributes. This is the characteristic of something, the symbol that is often associated when we think of a particular thing. For example, an attribute of steel is hardness. An attribute of rubber is elasticity. So, an attribute is something that people think of when they think of you. As a leader, one that wants to be respected, you need to examine your attributes, and be sure to demonstrate good ones.

Then there is aptitude. Aptitude is the natural talent that one has, the ability to learn something easily. That's why it's so important that a leader do something that they are gifted in, and not just because it's a paid position or something that's convenient. A person with a good aptitude for baking, for example, will constantly create new ways and new approaches to their craft. Someone that didn't have a good aptitude for baking would just follow recipes and do the same old thing, and wouldn't be very creative at all.

Next is altitude. A good leader can set the bar high in the area that they're leading. They are able to take the company, organization, group, or family to the next level of maturity. They are able to continually cause people to grow and mature in their surroundings.

This all makes for an attractive leader. People are naturally attracted to those who show passion, creativity, enthusiasm, and energy in everything that they do. It's hard to be a leader in a place that you don't care about, and it's hard to be a leader in a home that you don't care about.

Set Apart

Being smart in an area is one thing, but being gifted and using your gifts is quite another.

To be successful in any area you desire, you must be willing to set yourself apart. It may be necessary to divorce yourself from some of your old ways of thinking, and begin to search out new ways that are more appropriate for you to follow. Just because you were taught to believe something, doesn't necessarily make it true. Quite often, when we are young, we are taught different things by parents or teachers, who are simply sharing second or third-hand knowledge. Some of the ideas that we have received have no real merit; they could quite simply have been convenient ways to do things in the past. Or they may have worked for the technology that once was, and may not be relevant now.

Let's take raising children, for example. The only example you really have of parenting is from your parents. And if you took the way you were parented as a child, and tried to raise your children with those same skills, it may not work. Why? It may not have been the best way for you to be raised in the first place. It may not have been the best skills that your parents used to raise you. Plus, your child may have a completely different personality or disposition than you did, so the tricks and the disciplines used on you may not work on your children. Therefore, you may need to divorce those ways of thinking, and begin to educate yourself to raise your child in a whole new way—a way that may be more beneficial to both you and your child.

You could use almost any situation in your life, and examine whether the approach you're taking in that position is the right thing or not, or whether it is current or relevant. Look at your workplace. You may have been trained by a boss that didn't have a good attitude, and if you try to train colleagues with that same attitude, it may backfire on you. You may need to divorce yourself from that particular way of training, and create your own way of doing things. Again, this may be far more effective.

Can't Fight the Laws

There are laws that have been woven into the fabric of the world. And I'm not talking about laws as in *rules and regulations*; I'm talking about the laws that govern the universe—the law of gravity, for example. You can't fight the law of gravity. If you throw a heavy object up in the air, gravity will pull it back down. There's no way that you can cheat that law unless you replace it with another law.

An airplane, for example, is a heavy object, and if it were thrown up in the air, it would most definitely fall back down. But when you take the law of momentum, and thrust the airplane into the air, gravity cannot pull it down, as long as it's following that law of momentum. If you were to shut off the engines in midair, the plane would come crashing down. The first law, the law of gravity, would once again take over.

In order to be successful in anything, you must be mindful of the laws that govern what you're doing.

Throughout our journey together, we are going to look at a lot of laws. We are going to look at the laws of love: why these laws exist, what they do, and how they have been misinterpreted or misunderstood. We'll look at the good, the bad, and the ugly of relationships, and how love got messed up in the process, and what we can do to restore the balance so that it all makes sense to us once again. Through the process you will become more aware of the value love has in all areas of relationship. By loving yourself more you will become a better partner, friend, boss, colleague, etc.

3 Keys to Consider

As we journey together I want you to consider a few things. First, consider your own perception. As you read and consider the things I'm sharing, be aware of what you're reading. Consider how it lines up with your beliefs, or at least what you have been taught. Take time to reflect as you're reading, and see if what I say makes sense to you, and then consider how you will apply it to your relationships. I want you to read this book expecting things to shift. Expect your position to grow clear around you, and all your relationships.

Next, I want to ask you to really think about what you are taking in here. Don't just skip through the material, but examine it and begin to connect the ideas. Take on the belief that you can think and reason for yourself and form your own valuable ideas around principles that affect you, and your relationships. You don't need to be a victim and just take what is thrown at you. You can decide what happens and begin to take steps to realize this.

Finally, consider the significance of this material and the impact it will have on your life. Relationships are at the heart of everything we do, and more attention should be placed on how you structure and build them. If you have ever gone through troubling relationships, work or personal, you know the weight it can carry. I believe that they are worthy of your attention and you owe it to yourself to be the best version of you that you can be, and then demand of others that they treat any mutual relationship with you in high regard.

If you're ready, we can begin to dispel the myths around love, and have a closer look at how we can be built up from love. We'll discover how we can all experience amazing balance in every area of our lives: our romantic relationships, our personal relationships/family life, our business/career life (your livelihood), and our spiritual life.

Start attracting more of what you want in your life by simply being more irresistible.

Are you ready? Then join me in the next chapter.

Thoughts

Thoughts

Part 2

Time

"The broke person and the billionaire have the same amount of time; your use of time is your key to success."
— Jim Hetherington

Can't Fight Time and Change

It has been said that the only things in life that you can be sure of are death and taxes.

While that's true, there is so much more to life than death and taxes. There is so much more that influences us on a daily basis. Health is something that affects us at every stage of life. We can all probably agree that without our health, we have nothing. Even if we were the wealthiest person on the earth, if we didn't have our health, we would have very little at all.

The relationships we have with people around us are another thing that affects us tremendously. If you put somebody in a circle of friends that influence them negatively, their life will undoubtedly turn out negative; or at the very least, it would be a tremendous struggle for that person. On the other hand, if someone was surrounded with positive people to influence their life, their life would reflect that. There are a whole lot of things going on in our lives that affect us mentally, emotionally, physically, etc.

Choose your relationships wisely, because nothing will affect your life more.

I think we would all agree that death and taxes, while inevitable, are shadows of a couple of things that are really unavoidable influences in our lives. If death is really inevitable, it would follow that we should put more effort into staying healthy, staying strong, and trying to avoid death for a longer period of time. Since taxes are unavoidable, we should look for ways to strategize our finances so that we pay less of them.

Potential Must Change to Ability

There are two other things that I would like to suggest, which have tremendous influence over our lives—two things that cannot be altered or disputed. We can, however, be very careful in the way we approach these two things. By approaching them wisely and respectfully, we can have a more impactful existence in the world.

Those two things are time and change.

Let's first look at time. We all recognize that we have the same amount of time each and every day. It doesn't matter if we are broke or a billionaire, we all have the same amount of time. Not one person on the planet is given more time or less of it. Time, like currency, once it's spent, it's spent. With currency, we can get refunds, and get some of our money back on things, if we change our minds about the purchase. With time, there is no way of going back to get a refund, or to have it magically reset. Once we spend our time, our time is spent. If you go back to the original combo we talked about, how death and taxes are unavoidable, it would follow that we should be very wise in the way we spend our time. Why? Because we can't get it back, and we are uncertain of how much time we have.

When we are born, none of us are given a card that tells us how much time we have to spend on this earth. Anyone could have as little as one day or as many as a hundred and twenty years. There's no rhyme or reason as to why some people get more time and other people get less time. Sometimes it doesn't matter how well we take care of our bodies, or even the good that we do with our bodies. I've seen people who treat their bodies poorly live to be very old. They drink and smoke, and eat unhealthy foods their entire life, yet nothing seems to affect them, and they live a long life. On the other hand, we have all heard stories of men or women who take tremendous care of themselves, and yet die at a very young age. They eat well, exercise regularly, and take better care of themselves than other people around them. Yet for some reason, unknown to us, they die at an early age.

So, what do we do? We could do what some people do, and scream out that it's unfair, that it's a shame or a pity. We can say all these things. But none of these things would change this fact. We could say *to heck with it all*, and start to live life carelessly. We could start drinking to excess and eating poorly, and doing whatever we want, and just take the chance that we will live longer. Or, we could go the other way. We could become extremists with our health and our exercise routines, and so on, trying desperately to keep the Grim Reaper away from our doorstep as long as possible.

Both of these approaches can have negative impacts on our lives. One is fear based, and the other is just reckless.

The one way makes us very careless and, therefore, very disrespectful of the gift of life, and of others who value it. The other way makes us very paranoid, making it a challenge to be around us, and thereby adding unnecessary stress to others.

Since time is one of the things that cannot be replaced once it's used up, we need to do all we can to use it wisely.

All of us have either said or have heard others say: "I would help out if I had more time. I could get more done if I had more time. I would go to my son or daughter's sport event if I had more time." And the list can go on and on, can't it? "If I had more time, I would…."

We already know that we can't produce more time. There is no way I can go to my friends and buy 10 hours from them. There is no way I could say to someone, "Look, if you aren't doing anything special tomorrow, can I buy 10 hours of your day?" There is no way of bargaining for more. We just know that once we spend it, it's spent.

So, let's look at some practical ways that we can use our time wisely. Let's just start there. Before this section is done, I will show you how you can have an extra day per week. Would you like to know how to have an eighth day? Read through.

Using the word, *time*, as an acronym, I'll lay out some practical steps to use time more wisely.

T = Take Control

Acknowledge right now that you only have a limited amount of time to spend on this planet. Because you don't know how long your time will be, or how short it may be, start today by taking control of the use of time—because the truth is, no one is going to take charge of your time unless you do. People will take advantage of your time easily. For example, your boss or a client will have little or no respect for your time unless you do, and they will demand more and more from you if you don't guard yourself. And unless you take control over what you do with each hour, no one else will do that for you. No one will magically appear and remind you when you're wasting time or when somebody is wasting it for you.

Start to look at your time like money. The same way you have a budget for your money, have a budget for your time. Find something to do for every hour that you have, every day. If you do not assign something to your time, something will automatically assign something for you.

Have you ever noticed that?

Let's say you had an afternoon free, with nothing planned for those four hours. Isn't it amazing how, all of a sudden, one thing will come up, and then another thing, and before you know it, the entire four hours is gone? You haven't accomplished anything of value; something has assigned itself to that time. On the other hand, if you had four hours, and you planned out exactly what you were going to do during those four hours, everything that you had assigned to that time would get completed.

When you assign a task to your time, it's amazing how everything gets completed. It's like a goal sheet. When you write down your goals, and put action steps toward completing those goals, everything gets done. Even if all you want to do is relax for four hours, by scheduling it in, it gets done and that's a good use of your time.

It's important that you take control of your time, because without taking control of your time, life will just pass you by, without you noticing it. It will whisk by, and you will not complete the things that you want to complete. And not only will you not complete the things that you want to get done, but you will spend a whole lot of time doing what everybody else wants you to get done.

Have you noticed that the people who are very good at

assigning things to your time are getting lots and lots of things done? They are getting them done, and you're not getting your time back. Things are getting done on your time. Not only are they spending their time, but they are spending your time as well. When you start taking back your time, and controlling it more, you will then start expanding your life to the fullest. You will begin to get things done that you want to get done in a day. You will accomplish your goals and your tasks more easily, simply by being aware of how you spend your time.

Your time is your time, and you can spend it any way you want. But I'm cautioning you right now to look at your time and begin to use it wisely, because it does have an end. Your clock will run out. The question you need to remind yourself is: How can I use it wisely and make the most of it before it expires?

I = Implement New Patterns

In order to take back the control over your time, you're going to need to implement new patterns—new patterns of thinking and new patterns of approach.

You need to examine the mindset that you have toward time. Do you think about your use of time? Have you considered it much at all? I want to encourage you to begin to examine what you think about time. If you do not value your time, you will never take control over it, and you will never implement new patterns. Look at what you think about time. If you don't evaluate your use of time, you will continue the course you're going on, and you will never change a single thing. But if you're serious about implementing new patterns to make better use of time, here are some tips.

Tip number one: Approach. Starting right now, you need to take a new approach toward time. Recognize that your time can't be extended. It's not like fixing a watch. You can't just go to the jewelry store and swap out batteries and get another few years out of it. Unless you're having heart trouble, and need to get a pacemaker installed... well, that's a different story. In that case, you most definitely will extend your life. However, on a regular basis, that isn't going to happen.

I'm talking about taking a new approach toward spending the time that you know you have before you—which, by the way, is only the second you have right now! The truth is that none of us have any guarantee on time—no guarantee for the next minute, for the next hour, or for the next day or week. The only moment that you can be sure of is the moment you just had. That's the only moment you were guaranteed of. You know the time you have had behind you, and the time you've spent, but you do not know the time that is in front of you.

I had a dear friend that passed away while walking to the mailbox. He was retired, physically fit, and very active. One day, he had some letters to be mailed, and he told his wife that he was going to walk to the nearby mailbox and mail them. He got ready to go, kissed his wife, and walked to the mailbox to send them off. While on his way to complete this task, he had a massive heart attack and died, only a few blocks away from home.

The sobering fact is that we do not know how much time we have to spend. So, let's take a new approach to time, starting now, because there are no guarantees.

Tip number 2: Make the most of it. Make the most of every day that you have to spend on this planet. There are too many things in your life that will suck time: things like watching TV, sitting doing nothing, gossiping, and talking about things you cannot change and that just don't matter to your wellbeing. You can hang around with people that are going nowhere, and they will take you with them.

There are so many things that can suck time away from you. Don't let that happen. Make a conscious choice right now to make the most of every moment that you have, even if it's visiting someone that you really don't want to visit, or something that you've been putting off for a long time. We have all had those moments where we're visiting someone and we're thinking, "This conversation is the same old thing, over and over and over." Even in those moments, find ways to enjoy them, and make the most of them.

My mother-in-law was a wonderful woman. However, she had a way of getting under your skin sometimes. She had a habit of asking the same questions over and over and over again, and sometimes it just got so irritating hearing the same thing. As she got older, she moved into a nursing home, and she would get bored and would call around to her family; and often, if we weren't home, she would just leave a message. And the messages would often go something like this: "You're never home; you never visit me." Or she would just start to tell us about somebody else's problems (quite often the same one, over and over).

But you know what? After she passed away, I told the family that I would do anything to have one more phone call or one more voicemail. Somehow, after somebody is gone, what we thought was annoying, somehow isn't so much afterwards.

Make the most of each moment. Find ways, even in the midst of ones that drive you crazy, to find the best in them.

M = Make ME a Priority

As I said in the first point, under taking back control, you need to make yourself a priority. The truth is that nobody else will make you a priority unless you do. Unless you carve out time for yourself, each and every day, nobody else is going to make you do that.

Nobody's going to come along and say, "Bill/Jane, you're spending far too much time on everybody else; you need to make yourself a priority." Nobody's going to come along and stop you from investing in other people. Nobody is going to come along and tell you to go take care of yourself, or to not take on that other project but let someone else do it. This is not something you're likely to hear. You need to make yourself a priority.

I had a conversation with a friend of mine, who happens to be a chiropractor and a wellness practitioner. As we were talking, I was just explaining how busy that particular week had been, and how I didn't make time to go see my personal chiropractor to take care of some issues. I kept rescheduling the appointment, justifying in my own mind how I was working on a major project, and decided that the people I was serving were much more important than me. It was easier to work than try to carve out an hour so I could go and have a treatment.

My friend gently reminded me that I needed to make the time. And they were right. If I don't care about me through the day, nobody else is going to do it. No one else is going to magically appear in the midst of my projects and say, "Jim, go take care of yourself."

Now, my dear wife will often come and remind me that there are certain things that I need to do, but I still have to take charge, and I have to take responsibility, and so do you; because if you're like me, it's easy to dismiss those that are closest, and ignore them.

Isn't it amazing how a perfect stranger can suggest something to us, and we'll do it immediately? But when someone close to us suggests the same thing, we ignore them, or at best, reduce the importance of what they are saying, even though they love and care for us more.

The lesson here is to have a discussion with those closest to you, and decide the best way for them to remind you to do something. Find that way that works best for you to be reminded, and allow those who love you to use that way to communicate.

However, once you have shared the best way for them to remind you, and they communicate the way you want, don't you dare ignore them or get upset. If it's your way, and you've told them how to remind you to do things, then you must follow through.

Here's a side note: There is an old expression that says, "Familiarity breeds contempt." Familiarity can breed disrespect. We can become so comfortable and so familiar with someone that we actually take advantage of their presence in our life.

Day in and day out, they are there, and we become so comfortable with them that the respect and admiration we have becomes less. One of the most challenging things in any relationship is to not get so comfortable that we let disrespect come in.

If we don't treat each day as if it is the first day of the relationship, it can easily become the last. Think about it. Marriages fall apart, not because the love is lost but because the respect is lost, and not because people don't care for one another but because they fail to demonstrate it.

Why?

Because we become so accustomed to their presence that we lose respect. And the same goes for friendships, as well as business relationships or jobs. We become so accustomed to the surroundings that we forget to honour and respect those around us.

Remember that things can change in an instant—even being welcomed in the workplace.

Don't take anything or anyone for granted. Treat each day as if it's the first day! If you could remember this tip alone, it could save your marriage, long-term relationship, friendship, and even a work relationship. Treat every relationship like it's the first week of it, and you will continue to be a person that others want to be around and have around.

E = Execute Daily

You need to execute these things daily. Every day, you need to be determined to do these things to recapture your time.

Science tells us that it takes 100 to 300 days to form new patterns of thinking in our minds. That means that for a long period of time, we need to discipline ourselves to truly get these new things in place. We need to be willing to work hard to put these things in our lives. That means spending time scheduling them every week so that these things are locked in long term.

Before you know it, the new discipline you are working to put in place will be a natural part of your day.

Schedule Your Time

For me, a routine that I implemented to get my time back, was scheduling my week. Now I never start a week without taking out my weekly goal-scheduling spreadsheet.

On this sheet, I have the days of the week written across the top, with times marked out every hour, from 6 a.m. until midnight, down the side. Then I put the events I have through the week, in the appropriate hour through the day. I list the things I know that I have, and then write in the goals and action steps I want to accomplish that week. Throughout my day and week, I know what's coming up next. If people ask me to do something, or if an opportunity comes up, I simply look at my schedule and see whether it fits or not. I don't think about anything until it's time to deal with it on my schedule. This frees me up to stay focused on the task at hand, and frees up my mental space as well.

There are so many benefits to having this system, including not guessing whether I can do something, and having no fear of forgetting. It's all there. And it's amazing how much more I can get done in a week. I schedule my exercise, my time with my family and my wife, studying, appointments—everything. It's all there so that it all gets done.

This has become my routine, and it's a great way to get in the habit of taking control of time. This is the way that I implement new patterns. I make myself a priority. It's the way that I execute every day. I encourage you to do the same thing. Schedule your week, Monday to Sunday, from the time you get up to the time you go to bed. Schedule that time. It doesn't mean you have to be doing something major every hour. If you want to have a two-hour nap, schedule that in. This way you know what you are doing, and if someone asks you to do something else you can say "No, I'm busy!"

Remember, you can't buy time back. And you can't buy somebody else's time. You can't call up a friend and say, "If you're not using 20 hours this week, can I buy them from you?" This isn't going to happen. Once you have spent your time, it is gone. So, remember to use it like currency, and spend it wisely.

Recognize the importance of scheduling time and looking out for yourself. And use every hour you have, wisely.

Now, how would you like to have an eighth day in your

week? That's right, a full eight-hour day.

There's a simple exercise that I do with my clients, where you can start taking control of your time and, on average, find eight hours. That's right; on average, when I take clients through this exercise, they find at least eight hours that can be reassigned. And then, consequently, they get more out of their week.

All You Get is 168

Take a sheet of paper, and on top of the sheet of paper, write 168. The number, 168, represents the number of hours you have in a week. Now, write down the number of hours that you need to sleep every day for optimal performance. It's usually between 6 and 8, eight being the better target. Then, write down the amount of time you need to spend on you everyday. The time you need to pray, meditate, do gratitudes, exercise, etc. Remember you want to start taking care of you first. So how will you start your day? Next, write down the number of hours that you work every day or go to school. For most people, it is between 6 and 10 hours a day (remember to block in the time that you use for commuting).

Now, block in the time that you need for meals, and the time that you need to spend with those you love at those meals. Write out the extracurricular activities that you do each day. That might be going to the gym, taking the kids to their events, going for a run or walk— whatever it is that you do, schedule that in. Then, schedule the time that you watch television, the time that you use to read, or any other thing that you do in your day on a regular or irregular basis.

Now, total up the hours that you've just written, and see what you come up with. If you come up with more than a hundred and sixty-eight, you need to do a little bit of work. If there's some extra time, then you know you can be more flexible, and you can use that time in a different way.

I remember the first time I did this years ago, and when I discovered the eighth day. People don't believe it exists, but I'm here to tell you that it does. The first time I did this, there was eight hours that I could not account for. I couldn't figure out why I didn't have these 8 hours, and I couldn't figure out where I was spending that time.

As I started to go through my schedule a little more closely, I discovered where it was. I was watching an extra Netflix show every day. I added up the time I was spending watching this extra show, and I discovered that I had an extra eight hours every week.

That's where I found the extra day of work.

How about you? What number did you come up with? Did you find the eighth day?

Part of investing your time wisely and looking at it, is being honest with the way you're spending your time, and looking at ways to reuse it properly.

Try Not to Change

The other thing that I was going to mention was change.

Change is the other thing that will happen in life. Whether we like it or not, time changes things, and people change things.

New technology is being developed every day. In fact, multiple times a day, things in the technical world do change. New procedures and products are being produced every day. Ways of doing things, even at your job, are changing everyday. There is no way we can stop change. It's going to come.

The only thing that we can change is our approach toward change.

Even to stay the same, you must change. Our bodies are changing everyday.

The cells in our bodies are constantly dying and reproducing. The aging process is continually happening in our bodies, whether we like it or believe it or not. We can deny it all we want, but the truth is, time moves forward, and so does change.

Our responsibility is to not only make the most out of our time and opportunities, but also to adjust and change as things around us change.

That doesn't mean that we have to take on and embrace every piece of technology and every piece of production that comes along. We must recognize that times change, and things change, and in order for us to stay current and sane, we need to change.

I think of the Mennonite community when I think of change.

This is a community that has decided that they want to hold on to their traditions. They want to farm and live on their land in a natural and pure way. Many of them do not want electricity going into their homes. Most of them still heat their homes with wood that they cut and burn in a fireplace, and they cook in a wood stove. They have large gardens in which they harvest lots of fruits and vegetables to keep them going through the winter season. Many of them still only rely on horses to do the work around their farms, and they use horse and buggy for commuting. I find it amazing that they hold on to that lifestyle in the modern world today.

However, many of them have been willing to adapt to some of the new world technology in order to stay current and productive in the world today.

I have personally been to some of the farms that have no hydro going to the homes, yet there is hydro going to the barns. Not only is there hydro going to them, but there is also up-to-date, modern machinery so that they can produce products to sell. There are wood working and metal fabricating shops and so on.

There is still a lot of the old-school, traditional ways of doing things, but many of them bought brand new machines so that they can produce products and stay competitive in the market today.

This is a good example of how a community has stayed with their old traditions and not changed, but has also brought in new technology and new ways so that they can keep up with change. Isn't that beautiful? This brings the point home that in order to stay the same, we need to change.

Remember these two things, time and change, are going to happen whether we like it or not. Our responsibility is to do the very best that we can with time, and to embrace the change that is ultimately coming, and be comfortable with it.

Even if you chose not to change, and even if you refuse to get with the times and adapt, you will. Even if you sat on the couch and did nothing for the rest of your life, and resisted everything possible, you would still change. Your body is constantly changing. The cells are dying off, and new ones are forming, even as you sit and do nothing. You will age and change, even if you don't want to. Plus, others around you will change and that changes your environment indirectly.

If you plucked an apple from a tree, unripe, do you think it would stay that way?

No.

That apple will mature and ripen, and over a period of time, it will spoil—even if you did nothing with it.

It's the same with us; we will change and so will things around us.

The best use of life is to use change to your advantage.

Continue to grow and repurpose yourself. Find ways to keep yourself current in every market and in every relationship that you are in.

Treat every relationship and opportunity like it's new every day, and make the most of change.

Want to have better results with TIME? Want to accomplish more?

Reduce delay!

I learned this idea from Meir Ezra. When you eliminate delay, you will create more time. When you stop thinking about things and just do, you create time.

Think about it. Let's say you have a list of ten things you decided you need to get done by 10 a.m. What do you typically do? You look at the list, prioritize the list, re-examine the list, and then prioritize it again. Then you think about it for a while and warm yourself up to get going.

What has happened? By delaying, you've used up time.

Instead, just start. Do the first task, then the next, and the next. Don't think; just do. To the degree that you quickly move and get things done, is the degree to which you make more time—time you can then spend on creating, building, and doing more profitable things.

Remove the delays, and you will create more time. Don't use up precious energy by overthinking and overplanning—just do!

Thoughts

Thoughts

Part 3

Attitude

"Attitude can make or break a person."
– Jim Hetherington

Attitude is one of the most natural ways to stay healthy. By maintaining a good attitude, you can increase the quality of your life, the quality of your relationships, and the quality of your career or business.

It takes real discipline to keep a good attitude, however, when things happen during the course of the day or week, a bad attitude can easily creep in. The tricky thing is that we sometimes can't see these attitude changes come over us.

It is necessary to examine your attitude regularly in order to keep it healthy and strong.

What attitude are you wearing today?

Does it change daily?

Does it change according to the environment you're in?

For example, if you're at work, are you one person, and then at the club or bar, you're someone else? How about home—who are you there? And would your partner, family and friends agree with you?

Have you ever considered where you got your attitude from?

Have you ever considered why you have a certain position toward a person, place, or thing?

Webster's Dictionary describes attitude as a posture or a mental position. Your attitude merely reflects how you are positioned or how you posture yourself toward something.

So, let me ask, what is your position toward yourself? When you have a good hard look at yourself, what do you see? What do you think of yourself? How you feel about yourself will strongly influence your attitude.

Think about it. If someone has a low standard for themselves, how will they treat others? Good or bad? Will they treat them with respect or disrespect? Of course, that person will treat others with the same regard. If someone has a bad attitude, or has a poor opinion of themselves, they will likely have that same opinion toward others.

Have you ever wondered why some people have wonderful attitudes about everything most of the time, while others seem to have a dark or tainted position or posture toward things most of the time?

Some of it could be genetics or the way they are wired. Some people just have more of the good juices in their body. Some just have a strong mental disposition. You know the ones. The sky could be falling, the planet could be in ruin, and there they are, going around saying that it's going to be all right, and that everything is going to work out just fine! God love them, but sometimes it doesn't seem natural, does it? Most of us are riveted with anxiety and fear, but all they see is rainbows and ponies.

Apart from those supernatural humans, most get their attitudes from some other influences. Things like our family upbringing, our culture and schooling. Also, from the people we associate with and of course media: books, movies, videos and so on. These all shape our thinking and consequently our attitude.

It's Everything

> *"Our 'point of view' comes from some 'point in time.'"*
> – Jim Hetherington

Would you agree that a person's circle of friends can influence their attitude? How much do you think family influences a person's attitude? The thing that affects your attitude most directly is your environment. Good or bad, right or wrong, they all play a role in your attitude. The problem is that sometimes you don't see how your environment is affecting you.

Attitudes can creep up on you, and you don't even see them coming. A good practice to get into is to remind yourself to take inventory of your attitudes; and that as you take inventory, you would be willing to adjust your thinking, and adjust your approach to things as often as necessary.

On a scale of 1 to 10, how important is thinking? From the time you were born, you have been encouraged to think. From the simple games you were taught, and from the books that you were read, these all encouraged you to think. As you went through school and college or university, you were taught to think, not just on your own but to think the way other people thought. Most of what you learned was from history, or past records, so you were taught to think the way other people thought.

When you go through school, certain things stick out to you in different ways, and will affect people differently. For some people, when they study wars, most would think of the fighting and the struggles between countries. And of course, they would defend their favorite country over another. But for others, they might think of the injustice that perhaps was taken out on a particular race or gender. Others might think it was completely unfair that horses were used in battle, and be upset over that misuse. Every person, every personality, is going to take in things differently.

Science tells us that by the time you are 35 years of age, 90% of the 60,000 thoughts that you think every day, become automatic. Your learning becomes habits, and your habits become routine. Of what you do every day, only 10% is creative and new. While learning is important, it is also important that you remember to think for yourself.

Talking is important. It's the way you communicate with others, and the way others communicate with you.

Would you agree that it's important to speak up? Do you think it's important that you use your voice to communicate? But how many people lose their voice over time in relationships? How often have you seen somebody not stand up and defend themselves or speak out in a relationship?

You watch them become quieter and more timid as time goes on. You know that that's not who that person is; you know they have a voice, yet they seem to lose it in the relationship. It's almost like tape has been put over their mouth. They can't reason or speak out—they don't know how.

Do you think it's important to invest in yourself? Yes or no? But how many of you really invest in yourself? Too often, we see people in relationships that are more concerned about others than they are about themselves. They forget about taking care of themselves, about who they are, what their dreams are, what their goals were, and they just consider the other person or the other people as being more important. Too often, dreams are lost and goals are squashed in relationships because people are unwilling to invest in themselves. They have less confidence in themselves as a person.

It's as if trust is gone. Do you believe that trust is important? Do you find it challenging to trust? Your past experiences will dictate how much you trust in the future. When you were young, and if somebody hurt you or offended you, it would be challenging to trust. Past relationships are another way that you can lose trust. If a partner, a boyfriend or a girlfriend, betrayed that trust, it's hard to move forward. It's necessary to break those old mindsets. You need to create new ones moving forward.

Even in work or business it's important to look at your mindsets because every experience you go through in your career can affect you moving forward. Again, that can be positive or negative. If you had a bad experience with a colleague and left it undealt with, you could easily carry that experience forward and allow it to determine your attitude in a new place. Some of us have had that crotchety boss experience, and that can sometimes weigh on us and carry forward to other experiences if left unchecked.

It's necessary to undo the old beliefs. Would you agree? It's necessary that you examine your mindsets often, just as often as you examine your attitude. The only person that can change your mindset is you.

You need to be determined to do this. Another good word would be discipline! Both of these "d" words are not favored in the English language. It's hard to be determined, and it's hard to be disciplined, but both of these things are necessary if you are to form good attitudes, or anything for that matter. However, it is important to be determined and disciplined when it comes to attitudes.

How many would agree that you need to have good examples in your lives?

But let me ask this:

How many are a good example to others in their lives?

If you believe that having good examples in your personal life is important, then how important is it to be a good example to others? When you have good solid examples in your personal life, to live and to grow from, your attitudes will be healthy and strong. When you are a good example to those around you, you call them up to have good attitudes as well. Without good examples, you just go around and around in a circle, circles that generate poor attitudes. Without being an example, you can encourage others around you to have poor attitudes. Whether you mean it or not, it happens.

If you are not your best, others around you won't be their best. Who is influencing you in your circle? And how are you influencing others in their circle? Your attitude matters. Your attitude counts. Make it shine!

Now using the word ATTITUDE as an acronym, let's examine eight principles that, when applied to our lives, will bring a fresh new way to look at our personal and business relationships, our marriages, and of course ourselves. This will in turn keep us leaning toward being the best version of ourselves we can be. It's not a one-time task but rather an ongoing system that can be applied methodically to keep us on track.

When you get stuck in your relationships, as with everything else, you want to hit "Reset" and to continue.

Have your pen ready to write down thoughts as you read and let's have a look at the first letter.

A is for Adjust

Have you ever wondered what it would have been like to live in another time or era?

At some point, most of us have probably wondered what life would have been like if we had been born in a different country or a different time. Perhaps even in a completely different culture, or how about into a different socio-economic situation?

When we do this, however, we lose perspective on where we are, and we don't really invest in the life we have or the relationships around us. We can start to blame the environment, or our parents, or our economic status for everything that isn't right. Then we can slip into believing that people around us owe us something. We can rationalize that if we were born into the wrong place, then it's the world's fault, and somehow it needs to give us whatever we want or need.

Far too often, we settle into thinking that if only our circumstances were different, if only we had more, if only the other person (or the people around us in general) would treat us better and listen to us, things would be different.

The reality is that the only place we can start to make things better is right here. Where we are right now is the only place to start. There is no option to be reborn into another era, time, or economic bracket. The stork didn't make a mistake. We are here for a reason and a purpose. And the only people we truly have the power to change and control are ourselves.

What we need to do is adjust our attitude toward the people around us, and take responsibility. We need to realize that we are not the greatest gift to the world of relationships or marriages. If we spent half the energy working on ourselves as we do complaining or trying to change others around us, things would be a lot different. We would become people whom others want to be around.

What if we got into the habit of getting up each day, looking into the mirror, and saying, "I'm going to be the best person I can be today?" Don't let the world dictate what your day is going to be like—you decide. Decide to make it, and yourself, better in the process.

If you struggle with having meaningful relationships, take a new approach. If you're struggling in your career, or getting clients and sales, start to look at how you need to adjust your approach. Stop blaming others, take responsibility for where you are, and change. Instead of pursuing other people, do everything you can to be the person that people want to pursue.

You will be amazed at how quickly things will change in every area of relationship, once you adjust your position and thinking.

Look for ways to adjust.

T is for Think

From the time we were born, we began the process of thinking.

I'm sure our first thoughts were, "What am I doing out here! I was warm and cozy, and now strangers are touching and handling me in this strange new world."

Parents or guardians started by communicating with us, challenging us from an early age. They spoke to us and challenged our thinking; they played games with us and read books to us, all to make us think. As we got older, we started to develop the ability to reason, and began thinking on our own. Many of the references we have in our minds come from these early stages when people were challenging us to think.

Time to time, as we grew up, situations arose that hurt us or caused us offence. Our brain remembers those events, and forms systems to help protect us. For example, most of us have had an encounter with a hot stove or boiling water. We may have touched one or the other and were stunned by the feeling. Our brain remembers that, and from then on, we know not to touch anything hot.

By the time we reach 8 years of age most of our thinking patterns are formed. Those impressions from our early development years set the patterns for reasoning, and deciding what to do as we get older.

When we get into a disagreement with a partner or friend, what is the first thing that comes to our minds? Usually it's a recollection of a similar event from our past. We say to ourselves, "This is just like the last time," or "This is what happened before, and this is how I responded." The old thinking kicks in to guard and protect us. What we need to do is look at the situation and evaluate things from a new view, and ask ourselves, "Do I need to respond as I did before? Should I deal with this the old way? What new approach should I take? Is there something in me that needs to change?"

One of the dangers I see with getting older is that we can forget to think and apply new thoughts to a situation. We simply allow old patterns to take over, and we follow their "advice" without challenging them.

My suggestion is to look at each situation and, rather than respond by default, look at the response you're about to make, and ask if this is valuable to you now—should you respond differently? Recognize that your subconscious is only trying to protect you with its prewired responses. You need to examine the response, recognize how it came into being, and see if a new way can be introduced as you move forward.

It's crucial the we look at our mindsets, examine them deeply, and decide if there is a better way to approach a situation. As well, look at the habits you may have and see what the mindset is behind that behaviour.

Challenge your thinking!

T is for Talk

Talking is an incredible tool. Unfortunately, in relationships, men and women have two different approaches. For women, it's more natural to share and to express feelings and ideas. They can verbalize things more easily than men. Psychologists tell us that women have about 20,000 words a day that they need to share, and that men have a need to share about 5,000 words a day. There are exceptions, of course, but generally speaking, it comes more naturally for women to share and talk.

Men may not know how to share. Culturally, boys are raised to be rugged, not to cry or share emotions. Men are seen as weak if they cry or want to talk about their feelings. So, when they enter into a relationship, if they don't change their mindset, they will go on to be quiet and non-expressive. Women want to share their feelings and to know what is going on most of the time.

Remember that when men process things, they get quiet and think. Women when they process things they like to talk right away; men usually don't. When they're ready to talk, they will. It may take a bit more time for men than women. That's why I think it's important to have the conversation about the best way to communicate. If people were to get into the habit of establishing from the start the best way to express things, it would help in personal and work relationships, as well as marriages.

It's important to respect each other's processes. In relationships, we need to take a new approach to talking. Men, we must understand that keeping things inside doesn't help us physically or emotionally. We have to acknowledge that just thinking about things will not bring true understanding to relationship issues or concerns. And women need to realize that just because a man goes silent doesn't necessarily mean he doesn't care; he may just need more time to think it through.

Go to my website, www.jimhetherington.com, for a powerful exercise that couples, friends and associates can use to learn to communicate more effectively.

With practice, you can be a better communicator. So many relationships and marriages fail because of the inability to communicate. If we stop trying to be right in every situation, and listen to the other person, communication would become more effective. My friend and mentor, Raymond Aaron, says – the problem with communication is that people think it just happens. Communication doesn't just happen; we must work on the skill of communicating well.

If you're going to fight, why not fight for each other? Fight *for* the person rather than *against* the person. Have your friends' and partner's backs, try to see your colleague's or client's side.

Remember, we don't all process things the same way, and that's okay.

I is for Invest

The principle behind an investment is that whatever you put time, energy, or money into, will grow over time. For example, if you take five thousand dollars, and give it to a bank to put into a GIC (guaranteed investment certificate), after a period of time, when the certificate matures, its worth will have increased.

This principle can be applied to relationships!

Just as there are many ways to invest money, and different

levels of risk, there are several different ways to invest in relationships. They will cost something and may be risky. However, there are huge rewards to be had for those who invest wisely and are willing to risk a little.

Some people don't want to risk getting hurt, or losing, so they don't invest. They'd rather stay at home and play video games or watch TV than take on the risk of relationships. I would suggest that we take a good hard look at ourselves and know who we are before we start searching. We'll talk more about knowing ourselves and our values in another chapter. We'll discuss the importance of knowing what we stand for before we enter into any relationship, and how that will attract better opportunities and situations in our life.

Now let's talk more about long-term relationships—not classroom friendships or work relationships, even though these can grow and we do need to consider how and where we want to invest. After all, when investing in a career or workplace we usually go into that for the long term, and need to be aware of what we are doing. With personal relationships, if we want to attract the person we desire, we need to know two things.

First, we need to know who we are. We need to know what we value, what we stand for, and what the real deal breakers are for us when it comes to a partner. If we don't have a strong understanding of who we are, then anyone who comes along will do. However, I would suggest if they don't fit our future plans and goals, and if they don't value the things we do, then it's irrelevant how good they smell or how nice they look.

Second, we need to know who they are and what they stand for. What are their goals and plans, and where do they want to be in ten years? If you meet the most attractive person ever, but they don't line up with your values or plans for the future, why would you want to invest in a long-term relationship? What kind of investment would it be? The return would be little to none. Get to know them—who they are, what they believe, and where they are going.

And remember, there is risk. There is a chance of being hurt or rejected. However, if you take the time to know who you are and what you really want, and then begin to search out like-minded people, if you go slow and let things develop, and evaluate things as you go, the risk will be less. It's when people rush in without thinking and without a plan that things can, and usually do, go very wrong very quickly.

As with any good investment, be wise and do some research. Do your homework up front, and the payoff will be huge. Without doing the homework, you may just have to settle for less, or stay in and continue to play video games.

This T is for Trust

This is a huge area. Almost every person has an area where they lack trust in something or someone. But because we are relational creatures, most of us do want to trust.

When we were young, a friend may have stolen something from us, or a bully may have taken something that belonged to us. Maybe, when we were young and innocent, somebody took advantage of our heart, and broke it. Or perhaps someone in our close circle of friends abused our trust or did something to damage our reputation. The result could be that, as we grow up, we lack confidence in people. We find it hard to trust. This can be carried into adulthood.

As you get to know a person and see their values, directions, and goals, you lower your guard a bit, and allow them to enter into your circle of trust. Little by little, as you get to know each other, the guards come down, until you are in each other's trust circle. If you let your guard down too fast, you risk being too vulnerable. If you let yours down and they don't, it's the same thing: you become vulnerable to being overexposed. If the surrender isn't mutual and doesn't happen at the same time, the balance can be thrown off; trust isn't reciprocated.

Going back to the idea of having your own values list, knowing who you really are will certainly help in the trust area. If you aren't confident in who you are, it may be impossible for you to trust anyone, or for anyone to trust you. Know who you are and what you stand for. Don't go back and forth on ideas and values; know who you are and where you stand. As you exude confidence, you can receive it from others, and walk in trust.

These issues can easily be transferred into the workplace. Many of us are painfully aware of the gossip and backstabbing that can happen at work. We need to use the same cautions in our careers. When you meet new clients, or as a new employee, don't reveal your hand too quickly. Let people get to know you, and you them.

Remember as well, when you go into a new job or meet a new client, to examine how you are approaching the situation. Are you allowing yourself to be guided by old memories and not trusting, or are you weighing things out carefully and allowing yourself to trust in due time?

In my training seminars, I spend more time dealing with and reconciling past wounds. As we deal with them, we can move forward to see things in a new way. We gain a greater expectation for the future. For more information, go to my website, www.jimhetherington.com.

Go slow when you're getting to know others. Let them prove to you that you can trust them; don't just throw your heart wide open and hope for the best.

U is for Undo

Take a look at the areas in which you have problems with trust, and begin to reflect on how you can undo those areas. Start with undoing limiting beliefs.

Limiting beliefs will keep people trapped like nothing else. The self-talk that goes on in our heads can defeat us before we even have a chance, a real chance, to succeed.

Too many people have little confidence in themselves. Many don't have the ability to operate at an optimal level. And the sad thing is that many don't even know it! They have no idea, because these beliefs are the norm for them—it's all they know; that's all they do.

If you think negatively, you will become negative. If you think you're bad at something, you will be. If you think you're not very good, or not very smart, you may never become great or experience the benefits of being intelligent.

Henry Ford said that if you think you can or can't do something, you're right. If you think that you will never be able to do a particular task well, or that you'll never get good grades, you're right. The decision you make about something will become your reality. Stop thinking in the negative. Undo that thinking, and start moving forward in the positive, and make a change. Make a difference.

Having healthy and happy relationships is a skill. Being able to relate with people well is a skill, something we need to work on every day.

How do we make these shifts? By replacing the old habits, the old mindsets, with new ones; by replacing the negative talk with positive talk; by speaking powerful and positive affirmations, over and over; and by being consistent. Make it a daily habit to grow and learn. Write down your negative talk, and write out what you will say instead. Post affirmations in your bathroom, your office—anywhere you will see them—and then repeat them over and over.

I take my coaching clients through a five-step process to overcome limiting beliefs. If you want to learn more, go to www.jimhetherington.com to sign up for a free session, and discover how this process can help you.

Undo limiting beliefs, and make that shift.

D is for Determine

We need to look at our relationships. We need to decide how important they are to us. Then we need to decide how we will make our relationships grow, and how we will invest in them. We also need to decide to be likable and relatable at work and with clients. These are choices that will allow us to grow and that will take us to the top of our game. Most people at the top of any organization are likable, personable, charming; make the choice to be that kind of person.

It takes time and energy to form good relationships and good marriages. The more energy we put into a relationship, the more successful it will be. If we put little or no time into it, we will get no value from it. So, we need to determine how important relationships are to us. Look to relationships for not only what you will get out of them but also what you will give to them. It's not about just receiving. It's been said that you can tell a lot about a person by the way they treat others, especially when no one is watching.

We can all have good relationships, but we need to determine how much energy we're going to put into them, and what relationships we want to invest in and why.

Motives for building relationships can be very different. We might want to have a relationship for companionship or friendship. These relationships are strictly relational so that we have someone with us. In these relationships, we share special interests. It could be sports, it could be a hobby, it could be a club, or it could be our school or work experience, and so on. These relationships are strictly for companionship—to have a friend and to have someone to socialize with.

We can also have romantic relationships. These relationships are more serious, a place where we have a deeper connection. These relationships are very important, but we need to be aware of them as we go. I believe it's wise to guard our hearts and have clear lines around our relationships. This protects the other person, ourselves, and the people we love and respect.

There may be several reasons for us to have relationships, and we need to determine what they are. We need to determine what values we place on each relationship. In order for us to be a good friend, we need to know ourselves first. We need to examine our hearts and know if we are motivated by selfishness. We need to examine our hearts and determine how much energy we're willing to put into a relationship, and whether it's for the person or for something we will gain from them.

We need to keep ourselves in a circle of friends who will challenge us. Les Brown, the motivational speaker, once said, *"If you're the smartest person in your circle of friends, then you need a new circle of friends."* Friendships and relationships provide comfort, encouragement, and support. But they are also meant to challenge us. They should challenge us to be the very best person we can be. If they aren't challenging us but are taking us in an unhealthy direction instead, we need to get out of that circle.

In my book, *Your Relationship Rescue Handbook*, I have eleven "F" words that I use as a framework for individuals to figure out who they are and what they believe. It's also great for couples to use so that they begin to discuss their core values with the desire to strengthen their relationship. To find out more, go to www.jimhetherington.com.

E is for Example

Examples need to go both ways in our lives. We need to be an example to those around us, and we need to have people set examples for us.

To be successful in relationships, in any area of life, we need to have people in our lives who can be examples for us to follow, people we can look up to and say, "I want to be like that." They're role models. They're mentors. They're the people who take us to the next level. Without people in our lives to emulate, we will stay the same. Without a shining example, we would carry on and not be challenged to grow.

We may have younger brothers or sisters, or younger friends, in our lives. We may even have children. All of them will look to us to be an example of what a friend is to be, and what a person is to be like in a relationship. We may even have co-workers, a team or employees that are looking to us for direction. Many of us learned what relationships are by watching people around us. Our parents were probably our earliest examples of relationship. We gained a lot of knowledge, without even being aware of it, just by watching others as we grew up.

They could have shown us a good or bad example—either way, they set examples that we learned from as we matured. Your life is that to others around you, so be aware of your influence. For the most part this is the only way we learn about relationships. How are you positively impacting those around you?

When we have people in our lives who are good examples for us, and when we are good examples for others, we become the best person we can be. When we operate at our highest level, we draw others to their highest level too.

If we don't live as an example for others, we might keep them from moving forward and reaching their fullest potential.

The eight principles we looked at here can be applied daily and used as tools to help you become the best person you can be. Remember to write down what you believe and what you stand for, and begin to attract that kind of person to you.

Also remember to take responsibility for yourself and become the best version of you possible, and encourage others to rise up to be their best.

You can become a better friend and partner, and you can become a better employee or boss. By adjusting your attitude and hitting the "Reset" button, you will continue to be a person whom others will want to be around and that influences positively.

Thoughts

www.JimHetherington.com

Thoughts

Part 4

Heart to Heart

"You can lie to anyone in the world except the one looking back at you in the mirror."
– Jim Hetherington

Look in the Mirror

If you are like me, the last thing you do before you go to a meeting or leave the house to go someplace, is look in the mirror. I look in the mirror to make sure that my tie is straight, and that my hair is neat, and I smile to check and make sure there's nothing in my teeth.

Mirrors are an amazing instrument to get a true reflection of what's there in front of it. Unless, of course, you're standing in front of one of those specialty mirrors that you see at carnivals. You know the ones that I mean? The ones that make your head look bigger, and your body small, or they make your midsection big, and your head and your feet really small. It's all an illusion, but a real mirror will show a real reflection.

I learned a long time ago the value of looking in a mirror and having an honest look at myself.

Growing up, I had a lisp, and I was dyslexic. I found it challenging to learn, and I was often teased because of the way I talked, and because I was always reading the wrong words or getting the letters mixed up. By the time I hit high school, I was so frustrated and behind that I decided to quit school early in order to start working.

My thinking was that if I could leave this area that wasn't going so well and start something new, everything would be great. Have you ever had those thoughts?

As I started working, I soon discovered that my challenges didn't leave me. The voices of "You're not good enough," or, "You're stupid," or, "You'll never get it right," continued on here and into my adult life. Several times, I tried to better myself and to better my life, but it didn't work. You see, I tried to learn and finish my education but I had such a challenge reading and writing that I would get frustrated and quit.

Finally, in desperation, I remember going home one evening and going upstairs to the washroom. I was so tired of the voices telling me that I was no good and that I wouldn't amount to anything; so I decided that I would confront my accuser. I wanted to stop the negative voice that was telling me that nothing would change and that I would never succeed.

Standing there in the bathroom, looking in the mirror, I yelled out: ENOUGH!

You see, it was me all these years that was bullying and torturing myself. Sure, I was teased and bullied at school growing up; and sure, I had been made fun of during work, because I couldn't read a measuring tape because the numbers moved around in my mind. But I had to have a good hard look at myself.

Standing in front of the mirror that day, I took 100% responsibility for every choice that I had made.

After hearing all those negative voices for all those years, I took them on as truth. I started to believe the words that people spoke out to me, and I agreed with them. They said that I was stupid, and I agreed. They said that I wouldn't ever read well or speak correctly, and I agreed with them. That day, looking in the mirror, I had to own the false beliefs that I took on as truth, and silence those voices ringing through my head.

I had become my own worst enemy. I became so critical of myself, and I was keeping myself down by believing the false ideals that others spoke of me.

It's incredible the false beliefs we pick up, and how the mindset gets stuck. The only way to deal with these things is to face them head on and begin to replace them with a positive mindset. Start making shifts in your thinking, and in your understanding of who you are.

I chose to stand, looking in the mirror, and there were some amazing insights I got while going through this process.

Usually, when we stand in front of a mirror, we're getting prepared for an event. It could be work, school, or a social gathering. Either way, as we stand in front of the mirror, we are preparing ourselves.

But there are actually three things that we can see in a mirror.

First, we see the present moment. When we're standing in front of it, in actual time, we're getting ready to do something. We are looking at ourselves to get ready, to prepare ourselves, or to make ourselves look acceptable for the event that we're about to go to.

The second is the thing that we're going to: a future event. We are getting ourselves ready to go to something. It became apparent to me that as we get ready, we need to look at ourselves and examine our hearts, and ask: Is there anything in me that is preventing me from being the best person I can be as

I go to this event? What can I do now, looking at myself and change to create a better version of me moving forward? That's the part where we take 100% responsibility for who we are.

As we look at ourselves in the mirror, we can have a hard look into our eyes, reflect on where we're going, and prepare ourselves for that event.

The third thing that we see when we stand in front of a mirror is what's behind us. As you're standing facing yourself in the mirror, if you look over your shoulder, you can see the wall and the objects that are behind you. If you think about it, it's like we are looking at past events: We can look at things that have happened, and reflect on them.

Ask yourself things like: Are there events in the past that I need to forgive myself for? Are there things in my past that I need to forgive others for? Are there things in my past that I'm holding on to that are keeping me from going forward?

These are all things that we can ask ourselves as we look in our eyes in the mirror. Standing in front of the mirror while getting prepared for a moment or future moment, we don't think about past events and how they affect us moving forward.

However, I know that I did, the day I stood in front of the mirror and said that enough was enough. That day I began to silence the voices that had been ringing in my head and ruling my life for so long. Those voices were dictating my level of confidence and self-assurance. I had allowed everything that others said about me to control me, and it affected my self-esteem.

For me, that moment was life changing. And now I find that I don't have to physically stand in front of a mirror—I can imagine it myself, and picture the things that need to change, and I can work on them. You can try the same thing. Use the times in front of an actual mirror to practice examining your self, and as you get in the habit of doing this practice, you can do it anywhere.

The mirror is a good reminder. It's a reminder to look past the clothes, past the hair and make-up, and take a deeper look at what really matters. Look at your heart. You will never stand in front of a mirror the same way again. And you shouldn't. Get into the habit of encouraging yourself as well by saying things like "I'm amazing, I feel great, I can do this!"

Note that it may seem strange at first. You may be like me; you may feel a bit odd looking into your own eyes. With practice, it will gradually become more natural to take this type of inventory and to build yourself up.

Not only do I practice this on a regular basis, but it also allowed me to discover three key principles.

Values

The first one is values. We're going to talk a lot more about values throughout this material, but for right now, I want us to consider the importance of values in our lives.

"Our values will attract us to what we want and distract us from what we don't want in life."
– Jim Hetherington

Our values define who we are as a person.
Let me explain.
If someone has a low set of values, for example, lying, cheating, being dishonest, being undisciplined, and so on, what do you think that person will attract into their life?
Exactly.
The exact same thing. A person of low values will attract

other people with the same values. I had a mentor that said to me one time, if a person doesn't stand for one thing, they will fall for anything. It all comes back to value. What we believe and what we live out in our life is what we attract from the world.

On the other hand, if someone has a high set of values, what do you think they will attract? Right, again; they will attract people and opportunities with those same values. If a person values honesty, integrity, discipline, consideration, respect, and so on, that is the type of person that they will attract into their life. Honest people will typically hang around other honest people. Disciplined people will often hang around disciplined people; and disciplined people set themselves up in situations that will attract greater opportunities.

This is the importance of knowing what our values are. As I mentioned, we are going to talk more about values as we go, but for now, this will set the stage for why I believe it's so important that we understand and know what we value.

Before we go on, let me share a story that will help you see it clearer.

This happened when I was in high school. When I entered grade 10, I wasn't quite 16 and, by law in my province, I had to be 16 before I could quit school, and that meant I had to finish grade 10. So, I continued to go to school, but I started skipping classes and not attending most of the time. Basically, I was just putting in time.

An interesting thing happened during this time, which I didn't understand until sometime later in life.

I clearly remember making the decision that I would not finish school. As soon as I completed my time and turned 16, that was it for me—I was done. Mentally, I had checked out. Physically, my body was there, but I wasn't paying attention, and I wasn't a willing participant.

Within a short period of time, I remember meeting a guy, and we skipped class together. We were sitting in his car, behind the school, and he started to talk the same language. He was old enough to quit school, but his parents were making him stay until he was 18. Out of protest, he had also stopped going to most of his classes. He, too, had checked out, but he was still putting in the time.

The strange thing is that we had no common friends. He was two years older, so we had no common classes. It was pure *value* attraction. The value we shared was that we both disliked school; we were putting in time until we could quit, and we had given up on the school system and replaced it with a new value: freedom/rebellion.

Looking back at that time, it was no coincidence that that person showed up in my life. Within days of me deciding that my value was no longer there in school, I believe that my decision to check out had attracted that into my life. My value was in not attending or even being at school, and the next thing I knew, I had people in my life that shared the same value: We disliked being in school.

Take a look at the circle of friends that you're in. Do they reflect your values? Are they just a reflection of who you are as a person? That's something that only you can answer. I'd like to suggest that having a good hard look in the mirror, and asking yourself the tough questions, may reveal some interesting facts. These facts may be keeping you trapped in circles of influence that you are attracting.

They may be ones that are keeping you from the desired groups of influence you want to be involved with. Also, holding certain values may be keeping people from entering your life that may be of benefit to you.

Purpose

The next thing that I discovered was my purpose.

Once I knew what my values were, and what was important to me, I began to discover my purpose. I believe that each one of us is born with seeds in us. These seeds are our gift, and the very thing we were placed on this planet to bring forth.

When we place ourselves in the right environment, these seeds begin to grow and develop. It's like a seed that you would find in a piece of fruit. Take an apple, for example. When you cut open an apple, you will find seeds in the core. If you took one of those seeds and laid it on the ground, it would do absolutely nothing.

However, if you were to put it in soil, and then place it in the right environment and water it, that seed would become a tree.

That's the same with each of us as individuals. We all have gifts (seeds) waiting to be developed. Our purpose is unfolded when we know our gift. We begin to understand why we are here.

There are seeds of greatness, seeds of opportunity, and seeds of creativity—there is so much inside of us. However, we need to place ourselves in the proper environment so that we can grow. And as we grow, our purpose unfolds. We begin to see why we were created. Our gift is what we have to give back to this planet. It's only by knowing what our values are, and then discovering our purpose, that we can begin to see our gifts.

Once we know our values, and discover our purpose, we are ready for the third thing.

Success

The third thing is success.

Once we know our values, and discover our purpose, then we can begin to work toward success.

At this stage, I think it's important to define what your success is.

It's of no value for a person to say that they want to be successful—it must be defined. You need to have clear and defined goals to be successful. One needs to determine what success is, and what they are going to do to achieve that success. If you don't know what it is or how you will get there, you won't know if or when you have arrived.

For example, for some people, making an average income of $45,000, saving some money, and being able to purchase what they want, when they want, is success. And if that's your definition of success, that's a wonderful definition.

For other people, it's making an above average income of, for example, $150,000, and not just saving some money but having investments to grow their wealth. They may want to buy an investment property or run their own business. To them, that would be success. And that is a good definition of success.

For others, it's making multiple millions of dollars, developing businesses, growing companies, having multiple streams of income, and owning properties. It's accumulating massive wealth so that they can help others, and maybe never retiring but just living a lifestyle where they grow and develop their wealth. And that's an amazing definition of success.

It's clear to see that we need to know what success means to us. If we go aimlessly through life, and don't put any clear value to success, and if we don't understand our gifts or purpose, success will never mean anything. It must be clearly defined. Like a clear and identified target, you need to see it in order to hit it. Once it's defined, then you know if you are getting close to achieving it.

Sit down and have a hard look in the mirror, and ask the tough question: What is success to me? When you can begin to see what it is, you can then begin to put a plan together and develop action steps that will propel you toward that goal of success.

We're going to talk more about success in a later chapter; but for now, that's a good framework for where we're going to go with this.

Before we finish this chapter, I want to help prepare our hearts and shift our mindsets, to really begin to prepare to be successful. Being successful isn't just about money. There is a whole lot more. There's a lot we need to consider in our own minds and in our own thinking, before we can even begin to be prepared for success.

Sometimes we can keep ourselves from being successful. This may sound strange, but let me share a few points I gleaned from T.D. Jakes, that might help you understand.

Beliefs That May be Keeping You From Success

The first thing to look at is whether you feel that you deserve it.

This is one of the critical points that we need to examine in our own lives. Most people say that they want money and that they want success. However, if they took an honest look at their heart, they would look at these things and say that they don't really deserve them.

It's not that they don't deserve them; it's that their mindset won't allow them to have these things. For many of us, we are raised with the mentality that enough is good enough, or that a little is enough. It may be that huge amounts of reward are more than our mind can take in and absorb. So, we unknowingly keep ourselves from success, because we don't feel that we deserve it, or our own mind isn't prepared to receive it.

It has a lot to do with our self-image as well. A person with a poor self-image can't imagine themselves being successful and, therefore, will not allow themselves to be successful. They will just stay with the little that they have, believing that that's all they deserve. When success comes close, we act like a small child in the presence of a stranger. From a distance, they aren't intimidating, but the closer they come, the more we are frightened to be too close to them.

It's not that they are scary; it's that they are new and unfamiliar. In our minds it's better to stay with the little because we know what that environment looks like, rather than become successful and move into an area that is unfamiliar. The fear of the unknown and unfamiliar will cause us to reject success sometimes unknowingly. We need to get our minds familiar to success. Through developing a plan, getting around other like-minded individuals, and believing in ourselves, we can get comfortable with success. Believe that you deserve to be successful.

The next thing is that you don't want it.

You may look around and see other successful people, and see the struggles that they have socially or personally, and decide that you don't want that. You may look at successful people and not want the hassle of having people coming around asking for money, and asking for things all the time. Because if you became successful, you can almost guarantee that you will start to hear from family members that you had no idea you had, and from friends you haven't heard from in a long, long time, all asking for help. This is often a big reason why some don't want success. They think that life would just be easier without it, and they don't allow themselves to be successful so that they don't have to deal with those bigger issues.

Don't allow what you see happening to others keep you from success. With proper safeguards in place it doesn't have to happen to you. Don't disqualify yourself before you start.

Next is that they don't want to change.

Success will change you, and your maturity must change with the responsibility of finances and success. You may need to begin to associate with new and different people. Sometimes that change is what keeps people from success. It's almost a self-sabotaging thing. In their mind, they can't imagine changing, and so they won't allow themselves to be successful. In their mind, it would be easier to stay in the familiar circumstance of being broke, than to risk the change of going into unfamiliar territory.

Fear of the unknown can paralyze people and keep them in unhealthy environments. Examine your reasons for not wanting to change.

Maybe your fear of success is that it won't last.

Rather than having success, even for a short time, you would rather stay with the security of nothing, rather than risk going for success. There could be a fear of a failing or not doing it right. Rather than risk being successful, you just convince yourself that it won't last, and then you say things like, "I'll only blow it; it's not for me," and you just stay away from being successful.

The next thing is not trusting it.

Growing up in a certain circle of friends, class, or society, you may not trust the people in that new class because of what you have witnessed or heard. You don't believe you can fit in and be a part of this new circle. Rather than becoming successful, you choose to just stay where you are. You don't want people looking at you in a different way, or saying things about you, so you decide in your mind to stay where you are, because it's easier to trust what you have and know, rather than trust something new and unknown. It seems easier to stay in the familiar rather than learning a whole new system.

Or you may just not like successful or wealthy people. You may have a certain idea about them; that they are selfish, rude, or conceited. This may be part of why you don't want to be successful, because you don't want to be labelled that way.

Lastly, one of the beliefs that keep people from success is not believing that it's real.

Once again, this brings us back to self-sabotage. In our minds, we think that all this is great but it's not going to last, and that it's not really going to stay around. Therefore, we feel we are setting ourselves up for failure, so we don't even try. It's hard to imagine something bigger than what we've experienced before.

These are some mindsets that may need to be addressed in order to really have lasting success. We can define what it means to us in terms of money, real estate, or investments, but until we look at our hearts and adjust our mindsets, we will not be ready for success.

Preparation is the Key to Lasting Success

Don't believe me? Look at lottery ticket winners.

If money was enough to be successful, then anybody that wins millions of dollars in a lottery ticket jackpot should be successful. Right? Sadly, that's not true.

A group did a study where they followed lottery ticket winners for 12 months. They discovered that within 12 months, over 90% of the lottery ticket winners were either broke or in debt.

Why?

Because they were not prepared to deal with this new success. Their mindset didn't change with the money, and they didn't adjust their thinking according to their new success. Consequently, they spent all the money, and more, because they didn't know how to handle it.

We are going to look deeper at success, and the principles of success, in another chapter. For now, this will give you more than enough to think about and to consider. It will help prepare your mind to begin understanding more about success as we go along.

Some of the chapters may be challenging to go through. There may be some thoughts and issues that come up. If so, I want to extend an invitation for you to reach out to me for your complimentary 30-minute session just for reading this material. As well, at any time through this book if you find that questions rise up that you want to deal with connect with me.

It would be my pleasure to come alongside as a support.

You can email me directly at jim@jimhetherington.com. I would be more than happy to connect with you for a complimentary session, to offer further assistance, or to get you more resources.

But if you're good to go, then let's head to the next chapter.

Thoughts

Thoughts

Part 5

Balance

"Navigating life out of balance is like trying to drive on the freeway with only three wheels on your car."
– Jim Hetherington

Walking on a tight rope, stretched over Niagara Falls, there are two things you wouldn't want to lose: first, your balance; and second, your focus.

Everything would be done to stay on top of that rope! However, when it comes to navigating through life, few people give much thought to balance and focus.

Many will work long hours, deprive themselves of sleep, and avoid their family and other responsibilities for the sake of making money and becoming successful. They'll put great effort into their career, and sacrifice personal and romantic relationships, to achieve success.

There are four key areas that should be kept in balance to have real success. These areas are the physical world, relational world, business/career world, and spiritual world.

Physical World

The physical world includes the home we live in, the car we drive, and the investments we have. It would be hobbies, sports, teams, and personal activities that bring pleasure. It's physical fitness, exercise, and eating. It's also vacationing and traveling for pleasure and building memories.

Relational World

The relational world is all about relationships. It's your partner or spouse, children, and extended family. It would also include close friends, neighbors, and coworkers, people you spend time with or that you're responsible for, and anyone you interact with at any level throughout your day.

Business and Career World

This is your job, business, or career, where money is earned and wealth is created. It's where you train, learn, grow, and develop yourself. It's where you exchange time for money, or exchange services for money, and acquire wealth through building companies or businesses.

Spiritual World

It's the relationship you have with God, the Creator, and the Universe. It's what you turn to that brings comfort, encouragement, and strength. It's the clarity, confidence, and creativeness that is received from outside yourself to maintain inner peace and joy.

Sometimes when focus is given to one area over another, it's easy to lose sight on how to stay balanced. Remember the tight rope at the beginning? Lose **focus**, lose **balance**.

For many, a large percentage of time is devoted to career or work, which leaves less time for relationships, or to engage in the physical or spiritual world. When a lot of time and energy is applied to building businesses, and striving to become wealthy, a great imbalance can occur.

This is how people can become workaholics and have constant struggles at home or in other areas of life. They don't recognize the harm that they're doing; they just go about business. When problems become more troubling at home, the tendency is to spend more time away; being absent is more appealing. Eventually, it becomes easier and more satisfying to stay away from all other areas, and work, work, work.

This pattern can creep in slowly and be unnoticed. It's an addiction that people can find difficult to move away from. A workaholic gets most of their identity and self-worth from their work, or so they think. They need it to feel important and valued, and it's the only world they are truly comfortable with.

Through isolation, it becomes increasingly harder, and less desirable, to be a part of any of the other three worlds.

This mindset and thinking must shift in order to regain balance.

"You can have it all: balance in all areas of life and money!"
– Jim Hetherington

I'm not suggesting that building a business or having a strong career is a bad thing. It's extremely important to have a good career in order to enjoy life. The question to ask is whether you are sacrificing other areas of your life in order to have a strong business or career. Are the people you love suffering because of your absence? And is it worth it?

There are times in your personal and professional life that you need to make sacrifices. However, when it comes to a long-term relationship or marriage, remember your responsibilities to your partner, children, and friends. If they are the reason for you doing all this, they deserve to remain a part of you through all this.

A story was told to me about a man who worked all the time. He was successful in the world's eye but this work kept him away from his wife and son a lot. His wife endured this for a long period of time. Day after day, week after week, for several years of their child's life she accepted his excuses for not being able to spend time with her, with them as a family.

All of her time was devoted to raising their son and tending to their home. One night she had enough. She informed her husband that she was going out for the evening and if he didn't come home to sit with their son he would be left alone.

The husband made himself available and stayed at home with his son, and she went out. Of course he couldn't sit with his son and watch a movie or play a game; he sat at his desk and worked. His son came to him at the desk and did everything that he could to get his father's attention, and to have him do something with him. His father gave him papers to draw on, but this didn't keep the boy entertained long at all. Finally, the father took one of the pieces of paper that had a picture of the world on it and he tore it up in several pieces. He then instructed his son to put it together like a puzzle.

The father was quite pleased with himself and thought it would keep the boy busy for a while so he could finish some work. However, within a couple minutes the boy had it complete and was showing his father.

Shocked that this task was completed so quickly, he inquired of the boy how he had finished that fast. The boy replied "It was easy. On the back of the picture of the world was a picture that I drew of you before, all I had to do to put the world back together was put you together first. . ."

By trying to fix the world you don't fix the person; by fixing the person you can then fix the world. Examine your approach, and your motive for going after the world. Sometimes we spend so much time conquering the world, we don't realize that if we spent more time working on us it might just bring the pieces together more easily.

There was a period where I spent 2,000 hours, over a 12-month period, to study and earn more certifications as a coach. This was a huge undertaking and a tremendous sacrifice. In the midst of this, I still scheduled time with family and friends, and kept my time with them a priority. It wasn't always large amounts of time, but it was time nonetheless. And they all appreciated it and consequently granted me more freedom to devote to my studies.

Remember, quality time is more important than quantity of time. Sometimes there can be greater value in short quality times with those we care about, than in long periods of time where no value is really imparted.

The problem for some is that they don't even try to communicate this point they simply make themselves absent. If you would communicate your intentions, and listen when others express what they need from you, then a mutual plan can be created, one that allows you to focus on your goal but still keeps the ones you love connected and satisfied in the relationship.

It's easy to justify the long hours and the time that's needed to become successful. It's easy to rationalize all the energy invested in business and career. It's easy to create reasons why it's necessity for us to "fix the world." However, caution must be exercised to make sure that you're using *reasons* and not *excuses*.

A reason is a valid point on why something can't be done. For example: "I can't eat shellfish because I'm allergic." Or, "I can't go to the meeting tonight because there is a metre of snow on the roads, and they haven't been plowed." These are things that are out of one's control. An excuse, on the other hand, is something used to get out of a situation that isn't really life altering. An example would be: "I can't exercise today because I have a paper cut on my finger." Or, "I can't attend the board meeting tonight because I have to watch the hockey game." It's not life threatening; it's just an excuse to not do something.

> *"Question your motives for working longer hours, and check to see if you're avoiding home life or other meaningful relationships."*
> – Jim Hetherington

Keep the Pressure Equal

Imagine driving a car with the four wheels perfectly balanced and the air pressure equal all the way around. That's the way it should be: balanced in all four areas. When we spend more time and energy in one area of our lives over another, it's like one of the tires losing pressure— things become off balance. It's impossible to have complete balance in every area of life all the time because life is always changing and throwing stuff at us. However, when we put greater effort into keeping things as balanced as possible, it's easier to bounce back when we hit bumps along the way. When something major comes at us, we can regain balance when we have support from friends, family or God. When we invest in the other areas of our life, they are there to support and encourage.

What if you took one of the regular tires off and replaced it with a huge tractor tire? Imagine how the balance would be disproportioned. Not only would the balance be off, but you risk losing control and potentially causing damage. That's what life is like when it is out of balance. Without maintaining balance as much as we can, there is no support or backup from the other areas in our life.

Want a good exercise?

Take a sheet of paper and write down the four areas that we have discussed. Then write out the things that you do in each area, and put a time value beside each thing. Then add up the hours you spend in each area and see what you come up with. Are there areas that have an extremely high number? Are there areas that have a low number or a zero? If so, how can you bring a little balance back?

It may be necessary to have a mentor work with you to discover the next steps. Sometimes it's easier for someone on the outside looking in to help you see steps you can't, and then lead you toward them.

Now, please hear me, I'm not suggesting that all areas should be equal because, obviously, we can't spend 8 hours in each area every day—that's 32 hours, and we only have 24 hours in a day! However, check your math, and make some shifts to help balance the areas that may be dominating your schedule, and see if you should increase the areas that are lacking.

"To the degree that you achieve balance in all areas, is the degree to which you have harmony and true success in life."
– Jim Hetherington

I found myself in the midst of complete imbalance in my own life one time.

When I was younger, and running my own contracting company, I was putting in 60–70 hours a week. I was also serving as a youth and young adult leader, and mentoring for about 20 hours a week. On top of that, I had two children and my wife that I wanted to spend time with.

Life was very busy and demanding. I enjoyed running the company, and I enjoyed mentoring youth and young adults. I also loved my children and my wife, and was trying to keep balance there.

One evening, I was getting ready to go to a meeting, and something strange and unusual happened. I got myself ready, loaded everything I needed, sat in my car and turned it on, but as I tried to leave, I couldn't put the car in gear; I froze. For 20 minutes, I sat there trying to negotiate with my hand to put it in gear.

Finally, the only move I could make was to turn the car off and go back in the house. I called the people I was to meet, and said that I wouldn't be there. That was the beginning of a long journey.

What I experienced was burnout!

This forced me to reduce my construction crew to zero, and to stop mentoring and teaching. For the next 6 months, I worked one or two days a week. After a day or two of work, I was completely exhausted and worn out. I had nothing to give to anybody, not even my family.

After 6 months, I slowly got back to work on a regular basis; however, it was almost 24 months before I felt 100%. Still today, I need to be careful how I spend my time and energy.

My Caution

Before the burnout, people referred to me as the *ever-ready bunny*. I would work all day, stay up all night, and go on very little sleep.

Looking back, I noticed my thoughts and focus became clouded. When I was working at my business, I was thinking about mentoring and teaching. When I was mentoring and teaching, all I could think about was the business. It was a vicious circle. Trying to keep my thoughts clear, and keep myself motivated to complete tasks, was a challenge.

All of a sudden, my physical world, relational world, career/business world, and my spiritual world were one big blur. In fact, I wasn't investing in my spiritual, relational, or physical worlds—only in my career world. Very little time and energy was devoted to me, looking after myself physically, emotionally or spiritually.

Any person who is pushing themselves physically, emotionally, and mentally could quite possibly be one step away from burnout. It's crucial that you take time to examine your schedules and routines, and get balance back.

Here's a check list. Ask yourself honestly where you are:
- How much sleep do I get each day?
- How many hours do I work each day?
- Am I taking time for myself every day?
- Am I taking time for family or significant people in my life?
- When was the last vacation that I took?
- How easy is it for me to say no?
- Am I spending time daily in prayer or meditation?
- Am I eating properly, or am I eating on the go most of the time?

- Do I have clarity of thought?
- Do I find myself thinking of other responsibilities when I am working on something?

It's Crucial to Keep Balance

Would the people that know you say you are balanced and focused? Are you balanced at home, in your relationships, at work, and in your spiritual world?

The ultimate goal is to have as much balance and focus in every area of life as possible, to be in that place where you are the same person in your private life as you are in public.

> "There shouldn't be a public person and a private person.
> There should only be one person,
> consistent through and through."
> – Jim Hetherington

Would you agree that home needs to be a place where you can rest and be refreshed, and a place where you nurture and care for one another? If the majority of your time and energy is given to your business or career, it gives less time to enjoy with your family, which in turn doesn't allow you to support and encourage them.

Far too often, we give too much time and energy to our work and career, and there's little or none left to share with those who mean the most to us. Also, we engage less in our physical and spiritual life, and we become unfit.

Remember the rule when you are on an airplane? The flight attendants instruct you in the event of turbulence or a drop in cabin pressure to put your mask on first and then help others. The point is that you need to be in good shape to help others around you. If you aren't looking to keep yourself healthy and strong, you can't help others the way you should.

"Sad reality: Those closest to us, often get the least from us."
– Jim Hetherington

We invest so much time and energy in clients and business associates, and we keep very little for those closest to us. We go and go, and then have nothing left to give those around us at the end of the day.

What if we turned that around? What if we kept some energy, and gave it to those closest to us? Think about how that would build them up and, in the process, build us up too. Building healthy relationships, and having a balanced life, creates a better person. When you are your best you inspire those around you to become their best.

What if you scheduled time to pray and meditate on a daily basis? What if you got to a place where you rested for a solid day a week, and took regular holidays? This would increase your health and clarity of mind more than anything. Take time to go for a brisk walk in the morning to clear the mind and strengthen your body.

This would be time well spent, and a great investment!

Speak out gratitude. Every morning, begin your day by speaking out things that you're grateful for. Start with your health, and the very fact that you just woke up to another day. Then be grateful for family, friends, opportunities, and your community. There are endless things to be grateful for, and as you speak them out, your heart will be lifted up.

At one time, I used to exercise after work, but often I found I was too tired or didn't want to make the time. Then I started taking the first part of the day for me. Instead of going off to work, I get up early and invest time in reading, praying, and exercising, for the first two hours. Then I give myself over to my other responsibilities, but I start by looking after me first.

What a world of difference it made.

Your Future

What dreams and goals do you have? What hobbies or activities would you like to do?

Nobody is going to make the time for you to do those things.

Unless you take the time out of your day, and make them a priority, those dreams and desires will never be realized. Nobody's going to come along and make you sit down and invest in yourself. Work, clients and business are quite happy to take more of your time.

You need to make the time. You need to choose *you*, and make yourself a priority.

Would you like to get things in balance? Do you want greater focus?

What would that be worth to you?

I can help you realize the next steps.

As your coach, I'll show you how to take control. I'll help you see the next logical steps to start the process of becoming balanced and focused.

Together, we'll create a clear vision of where you want to go, and develop action steps to get you there.

Connect with me at jim@jimhetherington.com, to set up a complimentary session. In less than sixty minutes, we will create a vision and get you excited about moving forward.

Or you can visit www.jimhetherington.com to learn more about me.

www.JimHetherington.com

Let's get you driving down the highway of life—balanced and focused.

What are you waiting for?

Thoughts

www.JimHetherington.com

Thoughts

Part 6

The Laws of Love

"You can't fake love; eventually you'll be uncovered."
– Jim Hetherington

    The word, *love*, is sprinkled around in many different ways, and it can be quite confusing. Because we use it so wildly and generically, it's easy to misunderstand whether someone really loves someone or just cares about them. We can use the word, *love*, when we feel deep romantic connection or simply affection for somebody. The problem is that we use the word for almost everything else. We use it to describe our favorite ice cream: "I love maple walnut ice cream." We use the word, *love*, when we refer to our favorite movie, favorite book, favorite musician, etc. The word, *love*, is used to describe a variety of different things.
    It's no wonder that some people get very frustrated when we use the word, *love*, in any other context than the love we have toward a spouse, a partner, or a family member. Some people can become downright angry when the word, *love*, is not used in the right way. Some are of the mind that love is to be reserved for romantic or family relationships and not for shoes or bubble gum.

7 Types of Love

The biggest problem is that we only have one word for *love* in the English language, and that's *love*. There are several ways we can describe love or the affection we have toward something or someone; however, we tend to just use *love*.

When we look to other languages and look up the word, *love*, we will find that there are many words for, and types of, love. For example, in Sanskrit, there are 96 words for love; in Persian, there are 80; in the Greek language, there are several words for love, and each one of those words means a particular type of love.

We are going to look at 7 types of love in the Greek language:

Philia is *friendship* love. This is where we get the word, *Philadelphia*, the City of Brotherly Love. Philia describes the love that we have toward a friend or somebody very close to us. There's nothing romantic about this kind of love, and there's nothing to indicate family connection. It quite simply refers to the love that we have toward a close friend or somebody we like. It could be a neighbor, a classmate, or a co-worker. It could be somebody we play sports with, or any other type of mutual activity. It's the word that would be used when describing a relationship of mutual respect and admiration.

Storge is *family* love. This is the word that is used to describe the love between family members. It's the love that a mother has for her child, the love that a father has toward his children. It's the word for the love that describes a close family connection, whether it's a parent, a grandparent, a son, or a daughter, or even an aunt or an uncle, as well as cousins, nieces, or nephews. This is the word that is used to describe the close connection of a family member.

Eros is the word used for sexual love. It's the root word of the English word, *erotic*. This is sensual love. Eros love goes much deeper than Philia (brotherly love), or serge (family love). Eros love is the romantic love that is felt between loving partners. It's the kind of love that develops between two people who have taken their love past the friendship level, and who are certainly not relatives. This is the love that is demonstrated between married couples and those in long-term relationships.

Agape is pure love, God's love. This is unconditional love— love that doesn't hold any resentment toward anyone. It's the love that quickly forgives and doesn't hold any ill-will toward anybody. It's the love that is often referred to as the love that God has toward humankind. Agape love is the purest love there is.

Ludus is playful or uncommitted love. These relationships are casual, uncomplicated and undemanding, and can be long-lasting if both parties are mature enough and want it to go on. They are flirting and seducing, with the focus on fun. The problem with this love is that it can be mistaken for eros or philia.

Pragma is practical love. It's founded on reason or duty and long-term interests. It can be witnessed in political or celebrity relationships. Sexual attraction isn't of major focus with the goals and appearance being of higher value.

Philautia is self-love. While self-love is important it can also be unhealthy. Everyone needs to have a good value of themselves. The danger is thinking too highly and inflating oneself higher than reality dictates. There needs to be a balance to walk with a good self-esteem and self-confidence.

Words are so important and, as you can see, in Greek, and other languages, there are several words to describe something. It's important to choose the appropriate word or term. Over time, especially in the English language, words and their meanings have become less true to their original meaning. Words, over time, lose their zip and their pizzazz, largely due to overuse. The more a word is used, it seems that the true meaning is distorted or watered down.

Take the word, *awesome*, for example. In the early stage of the word, it was used to describe God: "the awesomeness and the splendor of God." Over time, it was used to describe something of major beauty, like the awesomeness of Niagara Falls, the Great Wall of China, etc. Today, it is used to describe anything from God to the awesome nachos that we had with chicken wings last night. The word has lost its original magnitude, and is used generically for almost anything.

It has become the go-to word to describe most things rather than things, or beings, of great majesty.

Breaking it down further, in English, there are other words and terms we can use to describe our feelings about something or someone. When we use the word, *love*, today, it's much the same as *awesome*. We use it for the love we have for God, and for the love we have for our spouse or partner, as well as for the ice cream we love (I'll place my vote for Maple Walnut!). If we were to take a little more thought, we could come up with words that would accurately communicate our thoughts. If we read more and took time to express things clearly, the words and terms would be there to clarify the truth we want to share.

My friend and mentor, Raymond Aaron, said this about communication: *"The sad thing about communication is that people think it just happened."*

That's the truth about communication. Using words and terms incorrectly and inappropriately doesn't help our communication skills. Just because we said a bunch of words in a row doesn't mean that anyone understood us. Taking time to think about what we want to say, and then choosing the words correctly, will take us closer to the goal of expressing ourselves.

Let's look at some other words and terms that can be used to express love at different levels. Can we agree that we express love differently at different levels? If we can agree on that, then we can look at these words and begin to get a grasp on the differences, and how we love and how we can express that love.

First, love is used when describing someone having a great interest and pleasure in something: Those guys have a love for sports; my parents love to travel; she loves the new fashions; I love Maple Walnut ice cream.

What is really meant is that they have a liking, weakness, partiality, bent, leaning, proclivity, inclination, and disposition. They have a real enjoyment, appreciation, soft spot, taste, and delight. Other words could be: relish, passion, zeal, appetite, zest, enthusiasm, keenness, and fondness.

Next is the love we have for family or friends: Those parents love their new baby; our boss loves his employees; my best friend and I love each other.

There is a deep affection, fondness, tenderness, warmth, intimacy, attachment, and endearment. There is a real devotion, adoration, doting, idolization, and worship.

Then there is the more romantic type of love, or the potential for romantic love: Their friendship grew into love; there is great potential for love.

There is real passion, ardor, desire, lust, yearning, and infatuation.

These are a few ideas of ways to communicate the feeling of love that you have toward something or someone. It can be just as clear, if not clearer, to those you are communicating with. Commit to use a variety of words when communicating the love that you have toward something or someone.

For romantic love, consider these words or terms: be in love with, be infatuated with, be smitten with, be passionate about; care very much for, feel deep affection for, hold very dear, adore, think the world of, be devoted to, dote on, cherish, worship, idolize, treasure, carry a torch for.

It's easy to see where the confusion can come in with the English language. When someone refers to loving their spouse, their dog, or their favorite sports team, it's easy to see why some people can become upset or confused.

The challenge is that we only have the one word: love. However, as you can see, there are dozens of other ways to convey the affection we have without relying solely on the word *love*.

Overall, it has become much easier just to say that you love something, because it's simpler than saying that you have deep admiration for something, or that you are very fond of something, or even that you like something.

One thing that we can do is to make sure we qualify our language when talking with somebody. If we have a relationship with the person, it's easy for us to express love in its simplest term, because that person would understand what we are trying to communicate. But if we are in a room or a setting where people do not know us that intimately, it is better to clarify what we are saying and why.

This can be done by just putting more thought into the words that we choose, and by being creative.

For example, if you were in a room with people, and you were going to make a comment such as, "I love the color purple;" instead of saying *love*, use words like adore, appreciate, admire, etc. It takes more work on our part to think of new words to describe things that we would normally say that we love, but it would eliminate a lot of stress than if we were to simply use the word generically.

Over time, people have just become complacent, even lazy, when it comes to the choice of words we use and how we use them. It's not something that is going to be easily corrected. It will take time and much effort on everyone's part to begin to use words appropriately.

With this in mind, let's start to look at some of the ways that the word, *love,* has been misused. The word, *love,* has been misused, and it has also been misinterpreted. Because it has been misinterpreted, it has also been misunderstood; and because it has been misunderstood, it is easily misrepresented.

In the chapters to follow, we're going to start to look at some of the *laws of love* and some of the *lies of love*. You will begin to look at how the word, *love*, has become so confusing. Because the word, *love*, has been used to encompass so much, it's difficult to really know its true meaning or origin in our lives.

As we begin to unfold these laws of love, it will start to make more sense to us individually. From there, it is going to be our responsibility to begin to bring clarity as we express love to those around us.

Keep in mind that as individuals, once we have learned this, we need to exercise it more by using appropriate words when describing love. We need to get away from being so lazy and complacent, and begin to use alternate words. This way, we can begin to correct the overuse of the word, *love*, and how it is interpreted.

7 Laws of Love

Most of us, by this point in life, understand laws.

Laws are governing rules that are in place to support or protect society. We understand the law of gravity. We know that something heavy, if not supported, will come down. This law is there to protect us because we know what to expect.

We all know the consequences of breaking a law, whether it's a speed limit or something bigger. Laws are in place to protect all of us.

Love has laws too.

They are woven into the fabric of the world. Love supports and protects every human being in one way or another. It's critical that we know and understand these laws so that we can appreciate love more fully.

When it comes to love, there are *laws* and *lies* about love.

Let's examine these laws of love, and see what new truth we can glean from them. Begin to line them up with your current belief structure, and see if there are any areas that need adjusting. That's the amazing thing about beliefs or mindsets: They can be changed.

Through new language, you can start to experience love in a new way, and perhaps apply it in areas you have never thought of before.

Law #1: It's for you

The number one thing to know about love is that *love is for you*. You are a created being that was designed to be loved. The Creator created you to be loved and, therefore, love is for you. It's not just for other people; it's not just for the ones that seem to have it all together; and it's not just for _____ (you can fill in the blank with your own words).

IT'S FOR YOU!

Far too often, people give up on love because they have never experienced true, authentic love. Or they haven't experienced love to the degree they want, and they figure it is just for others.

At the beginning of this chapter, there was a list of words

used in the Greek language, which all mean love. In the English language, we lump it all together and use the same word.

The problem with this is that someone may want *Philia* love (friendship love), while the other person may want, or interpret, the love as Eros (romantic love). Sometimes it's the application of the type of love we desire or want. Each of us needs to examine the approach we take toward relationships, and determine from the get-go what type of love the other wants.

If we would approach every relationship from a Philia (friendly) love, there may be less confusion or disappointment. If we could all agree to start with the basic and work up from there, relationships would have a greater chance to survive. It should be stressed that when a relationship starts with the philia love it doesn't mean it needs to stay there. Too often people want to jump to eros love because they don't want to be just friends. It's perfectly fine to start out as friends and grow from there; in fact, I encourage it.

The point to understand here is that you were indeed made to love and to be loved; it's in your DNA.

Know that love is for you and that you were created for love.
It is for you!

Law #2: It's for keeps
Love is meant to be lasting. It's meant to be forever. It's not something that is here today and gone tomorrow—it's for keeps.
There are a few issues around love.
One, love isn't a feeling.
For many people today, they love according to how they feel. We hear and sometimes use expressions such as, "I don't feel like I love them anymore; I'm just not feeling it with him/her; I don't feel like loving them."

Your feelings have nothing to do with love.

True love isn't a feeling. Love is an emotion at the low end, and an attribute at the higher end. We use love to express and connect with others; however, an attribute of God is love. God's essence is love. We can start to love something or someone, and we can stop, but it should have nothing to do with feelings. Once you decide you love someone, romantically speaking, then the commitment must outshine the feelings. Why? We are all going to have rotten days, or days where we aren't our best. It's completely unfair and unrealistic to "unlove" someone because you just aren't feeling it that particular day. Outward situations shouldn't affect our inward position toward someone.

If there are major changes, like abuse and neglect, that's a different thing. But just because you are having a sour day, it's no reason to not feel like loving someone.

Love is a law that is woven into the fabric of the universe.

Love is an attribute of the Creator. Imagine if God said, "I don't feel like loving today." All hell would break loose, and the world as we know it would start to crumble. Why? Because it's an attribute of God and everything that was created, including us, was done so out of love.

If the true source of love didn't feel like loving, we would be in a heap of trouble. How many of us act in a way that is deserving of love all the time? None of us. We all have those days. Yet we still want the Creator, or Source, to love us completely.

It's crucial to know the love you want, desire, and experience.

Many people play around with love and the emotions of the heart like it's nothing. However, it's meant to be forever. I believe that as humans, we can grow through the different types of love, and achieve the very highest love, *Agape*. It's our responsibility as humans to continue in the evolutionary journey, and to experience and love with Agape love (pure God love). This takes a tremendous amount of effort, as true love is selfless. Too often we witness people with a selfish or self-centred love, which is the complete opposite of agape love. Someone with pure love will go to the ends of the earth to rescue or help someone they love.

Love is for keeps; always keep it close.
It's not disposable!

Law #3: It's fulfilling
Love is meant to satisfy.

Real love is designed to allow us to demonstrate deep affection toward someone. It's meant to fulfill us at a deeper level, and allow us to demonstrate that affection in tangible ways.

Love is meant to be demonstrated in positive ways. Hitting, beating, and abusing is not showing love. Encouraging, building someone up, and showing deep affection is love.

There needs to be a clear sense of what love is, and there needs to be an end to the misuse of the word, *love*. Love never expresses itself in abusive, violent ways. In fact, anybody that expresses what they call love in violent ways knows nothing about love. They are probably angry and frustrated with themselves. Because nobody that truly loves themselves could or would ever express love in an unkind or selfish way.

Far too often, we hear people say, "He does this to me because he loves me," or, "She acts this way because she loves me." No! This is a misguided sense of love, and it's not fulfilling the deep need we have at the core of our being. This is simply misunderstanding what real love is.

People put up with this kind of treatment because it's what

they perceive as love. Their mind has been deceived into believing that something is love when it's not. In a negative way, this misunderstood love is satisfying. By this I mean that people can become so desperate for love that they allow themselves to be mistreated so they receive something. In desperation, negative affection is all they know and receive. I can assure you that this is not the love you were created for.

The love that I speak of as being satisfying, is the pure love that is demonstrated in positive, comforting, securing, and supportive ways. Love should never be received or interpreted in any other way—only if it encourages and builds up.

Again, because we are created creatures with this prewired disposition to be loved, true love is all that will satisfy. False love will not satisfy you. False love will only satisfy the greedy person delivering that false love. And as we'll discover later, love is never selfish or self-seeking.

True love fulfills far beyond anything that the physical can reach.

BE FULFILLED!

Law #4: It will cost you

I don't mean that you can buy love. It's nothing like that at all.

We all know that there is no real price you can put on love, because real love is priceless. However, what I am talking about is that real love will cost you emotionally, physically, and mentally. With love, you need to be all in.

You will need to put everything you have into love. It's a huge investment, which is sometimes risky and sometimes scary. This is why it's important to calculate and plan what you are doing. It's important to know what you value as a person so that you can look for and attract those same values in another person.

When you know what you stand for, you will begin to look for that in a partner.

There are several ways that you can calculate before entering into love. In my book, *Your Relationship Rescue Handbook*, there are 11 "F" words that I talk about so that you can create a values list, to use when looking for a potential partner. I believe it's important that we have a clear understanding of what our values are before we get into a relationship. After all, if you don't stand for one thing, you will fall for anything. If you know what you value, and line that up against the person you want to be involved with, it will reduce the risk.

Through knowing what you believe and stand for, you begin to look for, and attract, a similar person. This can save huge amounts of time and risk.

Another example would be buying a car. If you were saving your money to buy a car, as you were saving, you would be making a list of what you want in a car. You would begin to read up on different models and manufacturers, and define the car that fits. You would begin to test drive, and talk to friends and mechanics to get their opinion.

Then you would decide on the accessories and the colour of the perfect vehicle. Then, and only then, would you purchase. It reduces the risk of getting something you don't want, and it begins to get you focused on what is right for you.

For some reason, we put all kinds of thought and effort into major purchases like a car, but when it comes to relationships, we just jump in and don't give much thought to the cost.

There is a cost.

Those who have had the unfortunate experience of going through a painful break-up or separation will agree. Preparing to make a better choice will save you time, money, and heartbreak. Knowing the types of love and then discerning the love that is being expressed by another person will also help when you are making a decision to move forward in a relationship.

You need to put much more thought and planning into all your relationships.

Love will cost you, so it's better to do the work up front and make a wise investment. There's an old expression that says – you can pay me now or pay me later. Meaning, there is an investment that is necessary to have great relationships; you can do that now or try to take the shortcut and pay for it later. Up front there is some work and investment, but in the end, it will pay off. Don't think that the groundwork you put into preparing for any relationship is in vein, because it's not. Any groundwork you do to prepare yourself before entering into a relationship is time well spent.

When it comes to the affairs of the heart, always weigh out the cost before you invest.
THE COST IS BIG!

Law #5: It's noble and strong
With real love, there is nobility and strength.
It must be honoured and respected.

Here are some great synonyms for the word, *noble*: virtuous, good, honorable, honest, decent, generous, selfless, and brave. Aren't those great words? Who wouldn't want to be loved with a love that captured all these qualities?

To receive this kind of love, you must be prepared to give it as well.

In love, there is nobility and strength, and we can't expect to receive that kind of love unless we are equally prepared to give that kind of love.

Here are some words for strength: power, brawn, burliness,

sturdiness, robustness, toughness, hardiness, vigor, energy, force, and might. These are very masculine words, but they carry the picture of true strength that must follow love. Even though they are masculine sounding words, women have great strength, and demonstrate this virtue wonderfully.

There are times in a relationship, whether it's platonic or romantic, where we may need to be someone's strength, to stand in the gap for someone, to support and encourage beyond normal.

True love must be given with a great deal of consideration.

It must also be strong.

Great strength needs to accompany love. It can't be given with a weak heart or with weak intent. Rather, love needs to be given with strength. Then you need to continue to support it with strength, and be strong for the ones that you give love to.

True love is selfless and powerful.
BE NOBLE AND BE STRONG!

Law #6: It's the beginning

From the beginning of time, you were created to be loved.

From the moment of conception, and coming into this world, you were loved.

It would follow that as you enter into a relationship or friendship, there needs to be love. Even if it is Philia love, love and respect must be given from the start.

It's important for us to receive love in all close interactions that we have as humans. No one likes to be abused, and no one wants to feel disrespected or cheated.

We all need to be loved.

It doesn't matter if it's a simple friendship; there is still a deep desire for respect and admiration. This is why it is important right from the start to have good boundaries. If we don't establish the perimeters of the relationship, it will be starting on a shaky foundation.

In my seminars, I demonstrate this by having two people stand facing one another. They are facing each other, standing straight up, and they simply introduce themselves. Next, I would have them bow just slightly toward each other, and exchange more pleasantries. As each one introduces more of themselves, the other would do the same, until they are bowing to each other. That's the demonstration of good boundaries as you get to know each other you both surrender more details of who you are. Over time you would both yield at the same time. In doing this you have mutual understanding of one another and the relationship can grow equally. If one person or party reveals more, or all about them, then the other person may feel awkward, or they may feel compelled to share more but may not be at that place of comfort.

This, by the way, goes for any relationship, even in business.

Your approach to any relationship should be from the same position. As you reveal a little about yourself, the other must do the same, and so on. When one stops revealing, that becomes the boundary. When one continues to reveal more and more of themselves, and the other doesn't, an imbalance occurs, and the boundaries become confused.

This is the point of the demonstration: to start at the same position and lean in from there. From here you can also decide what type of love is being expressed and if there are motives. For example, if a man introduces himself to a woman she needs to discern if the motive is to just be nice (philia) or if he is after more (eros or ludus). In any situation, be discerning and treat the relationship appropriately.

When one person surrenders too much too soon, they are setting themselves up to be unfairly taken advantage of. They are exposing too much, without the other reciprocating. When one person gives too much of themselves too quickly, the other controls.

It's like playing cards and showing your hand without seeing the other person's. They have the advantage. It's the same in relationships.

Right from the beginning, you need to have mutual respect. As the love grows, you show more or you clarify it. It's also important to have respect for yourself. If we let our emotions get the better of the situation, and we show more than we should, we put ourselves at a disadvantage.

People desperate to be loved or accepted can often do this. They reveal a lot about themselves in the hopes that they will be loved. It's almost like showing off all you have, exposing your innermost secrets. It's vitally important to expose little by little and allow the other party to do the same.

You were created for love. Just as the Creator loves you, you need to love yourself. A powerful way to show this is by understanding that you are loved and valued.

Be wise when you engage in love.
START WITH LOVE!

Law #7: It's commanding
As humans, we are commanded to love.
As humans, we need love to survive and grow.

Without it, we are destined to break down. Many have experienced this when they have had a breakup or a separation. Inwardly, we are desperate to be validated by love once again. We will do almost anything to be loved, because love makes us whole.

That's why, far too often, people will return to abusive relationships—even though it's abusive and toxic, it's familiar. In that framework, the thought is that it is better to have the known than to have nothing or to start all over. The abused will often want to go back to an abusive person or situation, because it's less scary than starting over and facing the unknown.

We are to respond with love in every situation, because that's our true form, our true nature. From the foundation of the world, love was woven into it, because the Creator is love. In order for us to thrive, or even exist, we require love.

Love is insistent.

It will insist that we choose love in order to be fulfilled and successful. We cannot compromise with love; it will insist that we be obedient if we want success.

It is also imperative that we love. There are no shortcuts with love. What love calls us to, we need to respond to, fully and completely.

Love is imposing.

It will raise itself up and demand attention, and demand that we follow the laws of love. At its fullest, it is impressive. People may be impressed short term by imitations, but in the end, nothing else will satisfy with a lasting impression, like love does when it's beautifully and appropriately expressed.

Love is imperious.

In that it is the governing authority, it is assertive and attentive—not in an arrogant, self-serving way, but it is the crown jewel, and it won't be denied.

Try to have success without love. It will be lonely.

Try having all the wildest riches at your disposal, without love, and it will be empty.

The wisdom literature teaches that love trumps all things.

Love is also compelling, powerful, striking, and important.

I want to add a note here as we continue. I want you to notice that these qualities of love are both valid and necessary in the career/business world. Have you noticed that at all? Imagine if people were loved and supported with a clear, nonsexual love in the workplace. How amazing would it be to have coworkers, bosses or owners that supported one another this way? Just saying.

It's commanding in its simplicity, and powerful in its fullest expression.
WOW!

7 Lies of Love

What about the lies of love?

The lies are often accepted as truth. They are accepted as truth because they have been modelled for us so often; or, they are talked about so much that we accept them as truth.

These lies have kept many people isolated from love, for generations. Generation after generation, these lies have been passed on because of the previous generation's experiences.

The further we have traveled as a human race, from the truest intention of love, the more it has been diluted. It has also been misunderstood and misrepresented over time; so much so that we have lost sight of what it should truly look like. The expressions we often see today are selfish and self-centred versions of it. Far too often, love has been approached from the view of *"What's in it for me?"*

Take the single parent that experienced a terrible marriage, for example. Because their experience was horrible, they become a reflection of that for their children. Kids see Mom and Dad fight and argue, and they witness nagging and complaining; and because that's their only example, they begin to believe that this is love. They want to be loved, and can misunderstand the example they see in front of their eyes as love. That's why sometimes you will see an older sibling talk to the younger in an abusive manner. They see Mom and Dad do this, or they receive it that way from a parent and then express it the same way.

Let's take a person in the workplace, as another example. They engage in the water cooler talk, and they think that it is normal to expect nothing but heartache and games when it comes to love. They believe the experiences that people share, and they believe that when true love happens, it will look the way others have either experienced it or expressed it. People buy into the lies of love, and never explore the truth of love.

It's sad when someone young and naïve, looking for advice or council, ends up at the water cooler and gets their information from someone who's had a less than ideal experience with love. They are then fed with inaccurate information and go off thinking that it's truth.

What we find then is that people are fed lies, and they buy them as truth. They never question them. They simply accept it as normal, the way it's supposed to be. Seldom does anyone consider past wounds that may make people act a certain way, or their personality type, or the way they are wired as an individual.

All too often many of us have to experience things over and over until we start to figure things out.

There are so many factors that cause people to act the way they do.

People are wired from an early age to think, process, and respond in certain ways. Some things are conditions of environments, and other things are just hardwired in the brain. So, when something happens in a relationship, some types will act one way, and other types will act differently. When Bill says something about Betty at the water cooler, it may be in the way that Betty or Bill are wired, and how he interpreted the scenario.

To apply the conclusion as normal, would be a misinterpretation of love, but that's what happens.

Let's examine these lies then, and dispel them for what they are. Let's line them up beside the laws, and expose them for what they really are.

Are you ready to go?

#1: It's for others

For many, love has been so challenging and difficult that many have come to the conclusion that love is just for other people. They have come to the conclusion that love will never be theirs. They think that they will never master love, so they conclude that it's for others. It has to be for a special class. Love must select who it wants to share love with, and they resolve that it's not them.

Have you thought that love is only for others?

It's not! Love is for all human beings, and not just for the select few.

Love is designed to be applied to every area of life too. It's not just for the bedroom. It's much bigger than that. Remember how we talked about the 7 types of love: Philia (friendship love), Storge (family love), Eros (erotic, sensual love), and Agape (pure love, God's love), Ludud (playful love), Pragma (Practical love), Philautia (self-love). Love is for all of us, and available to be applied appropriately in all our relationships. It is, however, important to consider the situation around the relationship, our intention and express the appropriate love.

We can love our clients or co-workers, and our spouse or partner; not with the same love but with the love that is appropriate. One of the biggest problems is that the lines of love are easily confused. The lines of love get crossed, and that's why we think it's for others.

There may not be a problem with us finding love; it may be that we want love in a different way than it presents itself. For example, a person may have lots of love and support around them but because they don't have a loving partner, they think love is for others.

We may witness someone misusing love, and we try to mimic that approach. When it doesn't work, we think automatically that it isn't for us. The truth of the matter is that perhaps love is keeping you from imitating it the wrong way. Love may be keeping you from making errors. Rather than assuming that love isn't for you, examine how you are applying love, and see if your approach needs to change. Maybe it's not that love isn't for you; rather it's that you're trying to apply it incorrectly.

Discern what the appropriate love is in the relationships around you, and develop that level of love to the best of your ability. If you don't have the love you want, start to love those in your life, and you will see it start to grow and then expand into all other relationships.

Does that make sense?

Don't believe for a moment that love isn't for you. If you are a human—and I'm going to make a big assertion that you are, because you're reading this book—then trust me when I say: Love is for you; it's not against you.

Find out if you are applying it incorrectly or if you are receiving love from others in the wrong manner. For example, you may be applying Eros love when it should only be Philia love.

IT'S FOR YOU!

#2: It's a game

There are rules when it comes to love, but it is no game.

We have been examining these laws (rules) so that we can learn how to really play the right way, and how to play fair. Love is often treated as a game, a sport if you will. That's not love. If someone is playing with the strings of someone's heart, that's just destructive and manipulative. That's selfish, and love is never selfish. Love can't be treated like a game, where one plays with another's heart.

It isn't something where someone tramples on the other person's emotions. Everyone needs to play by the same rules, placing extreme value on every person, and respecting them as a person.

There are many predators out there that simply want to take advantage of love. I'm sorry to say this, but we need to recognize the gravity of the situation. Because there are some that think it's a game, they lie in wait for people they can prey on—the innocent; the weak; and the free-loving, trusting souls. They lure people away from safety, manipulate them, and take advantage of their gentle and loving nature.

Be on guard for those that prey. Be aware of this truth, but understand that this is not the norm. If you have considered taking advantage of love, only to try to gain position or popularity, re-evaluate your plan.

Love is not a game. I'm talking at every level of love. Whether it's in your neighbourhood, your home, or your work place, have a hard look at the rules you are playing by. If you are unsure of the rules, then expand your horizon a little and start reading more and more books on love. Re-evaluate your approach and make it your mission to find out all you can about how to love. If you have been lied to and manipulated, don't settle for a moment and believe that this is love. Take the same advice and

read, read, read. Consider your circle of influence.
PLAY FAIR!

#3: It's hurtful
Love can certainly hurt.

Anyone that has lost a loved one, or that separated from someone they loved, knows the depth of that hurt. When we grow in love with someone, or as we grow to care deeply for someone, our emotions grow together.

Love does involve our emotions, and as the feelings grow, our emotions grow more entwined with the other person. If you look at the heart in a romantic relationship, it's like putting two plants together in a pot. When they first go in, the roots are separate. As the plants mature in the same pot, the roots become more and more entangled. They grow deeper and deeper over time, and they get to the point where they are almost inseparable. If you were to separate the plants, you would need to tear them or cut them apart.

Get the idea?

That's why love hurts. Picture those roots as the emotions of the heart. When they are torn, they are just hanging there exposed, not knowing what to grab hold of.

That's all the more reason to play fairly and not take advantage of others. It's also more reason to spend time knowing what you want before you get into a relationship. Spend time getting to know who you are and what you want, and begin to attract that into your life. Don't settle for less than your ideal mate. Don't just think that anyone will do.

There are no guarantees that you won't be hurt, but it lessens the odds. All of us will more than likely experience it by losing a family member or close friend. However, when love is expressed and experienced properly, at least there are no regrets, and that will relax the pain.

Real love is never abusive and harmful. It is not supposed to be painful in the sense of being abused physically, emotionally, or mentally. That's not a true expression of love.

Don't exchange the truth of love for anything that resembles an abusive or harmful form of love. If you have found yourself in those kinds of relationships, that's not true love at all. It may be experienced in platonic or in romantic relationships. It could be experienced in the workplace or in the family dynamics as well. Remember what we talked about earlier? Keep good boundaries around you in all areas of relationships.

Don't believe that these are the best examples of love. Exchange these lies for the truth of love. When you do, you will discover that there is far more to love, and it's not hurtful and abusive.

LOVE DOESN'T HAVE TO HURT.

#4: It's not for sale
One of the lies of love is that it can be bought.

True love cannot be purchased. Love that has to be proven by buying gifts all the time isn't real love. It's a distorted and insecure view. True love can't really be purchased with gifts over and over.

Sure, gifts are nice, and we do buy things for those we love. However, true love doesn't demand these gifts. True love doesn't ask to be proven by gifts. True love is demonstrated through the support and respect it delivers.

There is an entire underground world that tries to buy and sell love. It's called prostitution. Don't put yourself in a place where you allow another to buy your affections. And don't try to buy someone's affections this way either. This isn't true love.

If there is someone in your life that is constantly buying you things or offering you things, just to keep you from leaving, have a look at it. Or perhaps you are the one buying gifts to keep someone else around and to keep them from leaving. True love doesn't need to be bought. True love respects and honours.

This can happen in your private life and in the corporate world as well. In the corporate world, if someone is constantly buying you things to keep you content to stay, you may want to look at that arena. Love should be freely given and received.

NO BUYING OR SELLING LOVE!

#5: It's weak and sappy

Love is often portrayed in movies and songs as being weak and sappy.

Love can and should be tender and affectionate but not weak and sappy. I think it's time to turn to the wisdom literature (the Bible) again, to understand the strength and consistency that is love.

Paul was a man who is responsible for writing a good portion of what is known as the New Testament; that is, the letters that were written A.D. (after the death of Christ). Paul, for the early part of his life, hated everything that was good. He strongly opposed love, and did anything he could to stop it, even to the point of killing those that believed in true love (God).

However, through an amazing encounter, he came to believe that God was indeed love, and that it was worth pursuing. He spent the remainder of his days proving that love was worth the cost.

In a letter that he wrote to one of the early churches in Corinth, he wrote these words about love:

Love is patient and kind. Love isn't boastful, proud, or envious. It isn't rude or self-seeking. Love doesn't get angry quickly, and it keeps no record of wrongs. Love celebrates the truth. Love always protects, always trusts, always hopes, and always perseveres. Finally, he said that love never fails.

There is nothing weak or sappy in love. It's tender yet strong, gentle yet relentless. It never fails and always defends. Strength comes to those that love and comes from those that love. When everything else fades away, love is there, holding things together.

Mature hearts can handle love in a respectful and commanding way. Love is far from weak, and it isn't for the weak of heart. You will find strength in love, and it will carry and lift you to your fullest potential.

NOTHING WEAK IN LOVE!

#6: It's enough

When two people are in love, they will sometimes say, "We don't need anything; love is enough," or, "We don't need that promotion or that raise; love is all we need."

I've seen people give up on their dreams and plans because they were in love. I've seen people walk away from advancements and opportunities because they were in love.

While love at times will make you feel like you can move mountains, love in itself isn't enough. With a true understanding of love, one would evaluate things with wisdom and not from a lesser position.

Sure, you need love, and you need to express it in a variety of places, like personal relationships and friendships, romantic relationships, and in the workplace. However, you still need to exercise wisdom and judgement.

Sometimes when love comes on the scene, everything else can go out the window, like common sense and sound judgement. We need to remember our core values, and value them in all relationships. Everything that you stand for and believe cannot be set aside because you think you're in love.

Don't compromise your values and what you stand for.

This is true in romantic relationships, and can be especially true in the workplace. When people start to work for a company, or start a new business, it's like a love affair. You think everything is rosy, and that everything will be perfect forever. You put in long hours for little reward. You sacrifice your personal time, believing that it is for the greater good. Then, all of a sudden, you wake up to the fact that you have compromised some of your values. You've compromised your integrity for the sake of the company's/business's benefit.

We have to realize that love isn't enough. It must be accompanied by wisdom and sound judgement in order to remain pure and strong. Love can't pay the bills; you will need to rely on more than that.

When entering into a relationship, you need to have a plan; you need goals and future direction. You need to understand that love will develop in a relationship, but it isn't enough on its own, this is going back to feelings.

There will be days that you may strongly dislike some of the things your partner does. You may dislike family, friends, and colleagues. In these moments, love that is unsupported may not carry you through.

You may not feel that your love is enough at that moment. Use wisdom and be sure to have people in your life, who have a good understanding of love, that you can call on.

DESIRE MORE!

#7: It's complicated

Love can be made out to be complicated. People can make all kinds of unfair and unnecessary rules for someone to follow in order for them to prove their love. People are asked to jump through this hoop, and jump over that obstacle, in order to demonstrate that they love the other person. Love can be made to be a gymnastic routine.

It's not needed.

There is a simple formula for love. This formula applies to all your personal and romantic relationships. It applies to your family. It even applies to all your business and career relationships.

Are you ready for this? It is profound.

Here it is...

Treat others as you want to be treated.

That's it!

If you don't want to be cheated on, then don't cheat. If you don't want to be called nasty names, then don't call anyone names. If you want to be respected and treated with dignity, then treat others the same way.

There is a universal law here, a law that is woven into the fabric of the world: Treat others the way you want to be treated.

Don't complicate love, but rather work on the love you have for yourself first, and then express it to others. Don't make love a gymnastic routine where you do a tumble and a roll, then a back flip and the splits just to show you love someone and don't make others do that to receive your love, just express it appropriately.

KEEP IT SIMPLE!

7 Things Love Hates

Before we go any further, I believe it's important to look at seven things that love hates . In order to really understand love, and to operate in love completely, we need to know everything about it. I realize hate is a strong word, however; we need to be ruthless with what we allow inside love in order to fully enjoy love.

Leaders, you need to pay close attention here. If you are a leader, a business owner, a boss, anyone in charge over people, please pay careful attention to the following list. It can be easy for those in authority to cross lines for the sake of production and profit. Be aware of the things love protests, because you can't claim to be a loving person if your actions don't follow the truth.

Previously, we talked about some attributes of love. We talked about the positive and negative things around love. There is so much that we can learn about love, but this chapter only touches the surface of it. Love was woven into the fabric of the world, right from the beginning. And there now exists a tension between love and hate. There's a tension between the understanding and motives of pure love and lust.

Lust is one of those words that I believe has been misunderstood because of its use over time.

Lust is usually used in reference to sex. It is used to describe the strong sexual desire that someone may direct toward another person, without any idealized or spiritualized feelings.

However, lust is any passionate desire for something. A person could have a lust for power. A person could have a lust for possessions or money. Any passion or desire, with impure motives or direction, could be considered lust.

Some synonyms for lust are the typical words we might think of: desires of the flesh, or sexuality. The following words could be used, not only toward sex but also toward any other activity in life: strong desire, lewdness, salaciousness, desire intensely, crave, and hunger for. All these words describe lust.

When our desire or passion for something is corrupted or impure, it's considered lust.

I'm getting my source from the wisdom literature, which is

Proverbs from the Bible. Now, you may not believe or follow the teachings from the Bible, and that's okay. For this purpose, I'm taking it as a resource for wisdom.

Even the great Jim Rohn read through the Bible and used the wisdom from the Bible in a lot of his teachings. He confessed that he was not a believer when he first started to read it, but he found the wisdom to be outstanding. The Bible is a great resource for wisdom. I'm not trying to convince anyone to read the Bible; I am purely using it as a demonstration of wisdom.

If we can agree that love comes from God, the Divine Source, Infinite Intelligence, or the Creator, and that love has been with us from the very beginning, then we should understand that love would have things that it hates or detests.

Quite simply, there are things that love cannot be, and there are things that love cannot tolerate; because if love tolerated negative things, it wouldn't remain love. If love is pure and from God, then it would follow that the love source would have things that it opposes. For us to truly understand what love is, we need to understand what love is not, or what it could not be.

#1 – Contemptuous/condescending/conceited eyes. Love hates these things, because they reflect a proud heart. A person's eyes are the gateway to their soul. Therefore, if our eyes are reflecting a poor image, then what is inside cannot be pure either.

#2 – A lying tongue. This reflects the motives of the heart, and also exposes what is in the heart. If a heart is pure, then there is nothing deceitful in it.

#3 – Hands that shed innocent blood. Not only are we talking about murder, we are also talking about anyone who willingly destroys the prosperity of any other innocent person. Killing somebody's hopes, dreams, or possibilities is just as wrong as murder.

#4 – A heart that devises impure plans. This means willingly and knowingly creating a plan to deceive or mislead others in order to profit from them, or to secretly plan or maneuver things to benefit from others failing.

#5 – Feet that are quick to do wrong. Love hates willing participants that join forces with others to harm or take advantage of something or someone.

#6 – A false witness that pours out lies. We all understand and know that lying is wrong, but to lie to discredit someone is worse. And not only that, but to do so to profit is worse still.

#7 – A person that stirs up friction among others. This is someone that willingly and knowingly causes disagreement, division, or conflict for any motive, whether for sport or profit.

Manifest love through everything you do, because this is how people will define you. You are defined by what you choose to do, not by what you know or who you think you are.

What you think is irrelevant. You need to demonstrate who you are.

This goes for every arena in life: your home life, your business or career life, and your private life. We need to be the same person in public and private. There cannot be a separation of who we are; consistency is key. Become the same person, no matter who's watching.

The greatest way to demonstrate this is by showing how you love. It takes time and discipline. We all continue to be refined every day; or at least, we should. Over time, the things in our heart will become purer and purer.

You can also look at it this way: Your life is defined by what you hate.

Love, or God, is defined partly by what is hated. We learned a few of the things that God hates, from the list above. So, let me ask you. What things do you hate?

It's these things that will define you. You need to decide. What habits will you form? Your future is determined by your habits. If you choose to do any of the things listed above, then your future will be defined by them.

If, on the other hand, you choose to be generous, respectful, and disciplined, then your future will be defined that way.

Does that make sense? Leaders, did you catch these things? How did you line up?

If there are any questions that come up as you read this material, I encourage you to reach out to me, I'm available for you at jim@jimhetherington.com.

Although, if you are good, let's continue.

7 Layers of Love

Now, let's have a look at the layers of love. Look at what really holds love up.

What gives love the strength it has and what it demands? What are we responsible to bring if we are to live a life of love?

Remember, LOVE gives, and LUST (envy) takes. Many relationships, partnerships, and marriages can operate in lust, and for a while, it will look like love because there is a strong desire or passion. They may appear the same on the outside, but it's the motive of the heart that tells the truth. That's why it is so important to know—to really know—the people we enter into any relationship with. Take the time and discern the underlying motives of the heart. In my book, *Your Relationship Rescue Handbook*, I examine 11 "F" words to challenge the reader to look at what they value in each of these areas. They are key to know before entering into a relationship, and are also helpful to know even if you are in a relationship.

In the work environment, it's the same thing. A new job or career can seem exciting, and we are all for starting this new thing. It may not be what we want to do long-term, but because it's new and exciting, we can fake true passion for it. We can appear to be exceptionally good at everything we are taking on, but it may not be passion—it might only be lust. We may only want the position to take us to where we want to be. To everyone around us, it may look like the very thing we were made for.

The layers of love could be likened to the support structure under a large high-rise building. For the building to be supported properly, and for it to be built to the height the designer wants it to go, that sub-structure must contain certain elements. Love, too, must have certain elements for it to support you, your growth, relationships, and partnerships.

Skipping a step may be fatal to the design of love. Compromising a step will surely weaken the support, and could potentially affect our growth. This is the reason that it's important to take inventory over our lives often.

Taking time to reflect on our lives is vitally important to maintain healthy and strong relationships. The stronger the underlying sub-structure in our lives, the higher we can build. By paying close attention to details, and to everything that we put into our sub-structure, we will be able to grow higher, and have even greater success in everything we do.

A lot of people don't think that relationships really matter when it comes to business or career success. This couldn't be further from the truth. You can't treat people poorly and expect to be successful. The stronger our relationships are, and the better we can relate to others personally, the greater the opportunities we will have for true success. People that can master themselves, master relationships at every level, and have the knowledge and wisdom for their particular field, are invaluable; the sky is the limit.

Let's examine the layers of love, and look at how we need to build this sub-structure so that we can have the massive success we desire in every area in life.

#1 TRUTH – Love is always truthful and doesn't lie.

You may be familiar with the line, "And the truth will set you free," and it's true.

We learned from the previous list that love hates lying, so it would follow that love must be truthful. In order to remain truthful, we need to sacrifice. We can't allow our integrity to slip or fall.

If we want to remain truthful, we need to commit to never put ourselves in a place where we are tempted to compromise telling the truth. To remain truthful, we have to guard our heart and never allow ourselves to be placed in any compromising place.

Love must be established on truth because there is freedom in truth, and only bondage and confusion in lies.

#2 STRENGTH – There is great power that comes from real love. Love is full of conviction, and is upright and morally correct.

The strength that fills us from true love is reflected in our character. It builds others up and encourages them at every turn. Love is giving and causes unity, and where there is unity, there is strength.

Strength gives the capacity of an object or substance to withstand great force or pressure. Love keeps us strong when the pressure is on. Life can deal some harsh blows, but love can withstand the pressure. It can keep us up when the pressure is on, because it can push back.

There's gentleness in the strength of love, but don't underestimate the power that comes from love.

#3 GRACE – Love is gracious. Grace is elegance, poise, and charm.

It is courtesy, politeness, manners, propriety, respect, consideration, thoughtfulness, diplomacy, and honor; it is distinguishing, glorifying, and elevating. Grace is also God's unwarranted favour.

When we walk in grace, and add grace to every relationship we are involved in, we invite God's favour and divine influence. We need this goodness poured out fresh every day.

Without grace, we are walking in enmity and cruelty. So, extend grace; it's a crucial layer of love.

#4 BEAUTY – Love is majestic and gorgeous when displayed in its fullest.

The word, *beauty*, means: a combination of qualities, such as shape, color, or form, which pleases the aesthetic senses, especially the sight. When we think of beauty, it's something that we see.

Love is manifested in the lives of those that truly exhibit love, both male and female. Love is neither masculine nor feminine. Love is love, and is demonstrated in the quality that shines out, regardless if you're male or female. Love displayed in beauty is a powerful thing.

There is an amazing fragrance that love emits, and one knows when they are in the presence of true love.

#5 INVITING – Love is always waiting, with arms wide open, to not only receive others and embrace them but to also give.

Love is always ready to give encouragement and support to those in need of it. When you receive an invitation from someone, you have a sense of belonging and connectedness. When you are invited to an event for business, you feel valued and honoured. That's love in its truest form, inviting and welcoming.

Always be open to receive and encourage others, never closed off and unwilling to include.

Love is inclusiveness.

#6 AUTHENTIC – Authentic means to be of undisputed origin; to be genuine, original, real, actual, veritable.

There is nothing false or pretentious with love. Love is genuine and real. It has no reason to be otherwise. To be authentic in love is to always be yourself.

Allow love to pour out of you naturally. Don't push or force love. Only allow it to flow out of you as naturally as breathing.

When love is forced, it will start to look like a copy. You don't want to copy anyone because it will look like you are trying.

Forced love always looks phony.

#7 ETERNAL – Love was established in the beginning of the world, and because it is woven into the fabric of the world, it is everlasting and will never run out. Because there is no end to love, there is no fear of running out, and there shouldn't be any fear that someone will get more than you.

All the love you desire will be there. Every one of us could demand a double portion, and it would be there because it's eternal, love will never run out.

Just as the sun rises each day, so does the everlasting light of love.

Now that we've looked at all the different laws, lies, and layers of love, the questions still remain.

How do we implement love in our life?

How do we go from being knowers of love to doers of love? The answer, in the simplest form, is choose!

The bottom line is that love is a choice. It's the same as hate being a choice, disrespect being a choice, and anger and negativity being a choice. These are all choices.

The fascinating thing is that we cannot carry a positive and negative emotion at the same time. It's structurally impossible for us to hate and to love simultaneously.

The object is to choose.

When something comes up in our lives, and we want to respond in a negative way, we have to choose to do the opposite thing. When someone lashes out at us, our immediate response may be to lash back.

Instead, by choosing to be positive and encouraging, we can defuse any situation. It all comes down to a choice.

When something negative comes toward you, simply choose to smile, and endorphins will instantly be released into your mind. They will start to flood through your body and create a whole new feeling.

But it starts with a choice.

Choose to put these laws in place. Choose daily to walk out in the positive. Daily begin to walk out in these different attributes of love. And choose daily to refuse to entertain the things that love hates.

Are you finding this a struggle?

You are welcome to reach out to me. I would be happy to discuss any of these laws, lies, or layers with you. I'll work with you to create a plan moving forward. Plus, I will support you in creating a system for your life.

Go to jim@jimhetherington.com, and let's set up a time where we can discuss things further.

I'm happy to help.

Thoughts

Thoughts

Part 7

Success Principles

"In order to become successful, it's necessary to define your success."
— Jim Hetherington

Define Your Success

Without defining success, you won't know what it is or whether you have made it or not. It's like trying to hit a target that you cannot see. Without clearly defined goals and clearly defined action steps for each of those goals, you will not reach success. You have to identify it to make it.

Success is different for every person.

For some, making an average income of $50,000 a year, and investing in retirement savings and retiring at age 65, is success. For others, success is making above average income, say $150,000, having some investments like real estate or in businesses, and putting away some money and maybe retiring at 55 or 60 years of age. Both of these are legitimate successes.

Still, for others, their definition of success is making multiple millions of dollars, building companies and owning businesses, having large investments, and never retiring but living a life where they manage their wealth and pass it on for their family's future.

The real problem is that many of us never define success.

We just go about life taking what comes, giving what we have to give, and hoping there's something left over at the end. That's just existing; that isn't success. That's just throwing your hands up in the air and hoping for the best.

VALUES-PURPOSE-SUCCESS

I have always taught that there are three main principles that will get them on this pathway. First, you need to know what your values are; then you need to discover your purpose, and then define your success.

We need to know what we value because, as the old expression goes, if you don't stand for one thing, you will fall for anything. Having a clear set of values demonstrates to people what we accept as being right and what we reject as being wrong. People can gauge our character by what we stand for. It gives us confidence and builds our self-esteem when we know in our heart of hearts what we stand for.

As we form our values and start walking in line with them it tells the world who we are. When we choose our core values, and choose the people that we want to have in our lives, then we will begin to discover our true identity. Our identity is formed as we align with what we stand for. When people think of a particular value, they think of you.

Knowing what we value will attract opportunities and people into our lives. If we have a low set of values, then we will attract low things.

Let's say that our values are lying, cheating, being undisciplined, not respecting others, and just taking what we want. What do you think those values will attract? Exactly. They will attract the people and opportunities that line up with those same values. Our circle of influence would be very shallow, and we would share it with likeminded people.

On the other hand, if we value honesty, integrity, discipline, respect, caring, and looking out for others, what will be attracted into our lives? Right, again; we will attract people and opportunities that reflect those values. What a person thinks on they will become. The very values you stand for are exactly who and what you will attract into your life.

I believe it's imperative that people understand this before they enter into relationships of any kind. If they know what they value and what they are looking for, then they are going to attract amazing people into their lives, and attract better opportunities.

It is the same in business. If we have high standards for what we will accept, and for what we will and won't do, then we will attract likeminded people. We will be attracted to higher quality people that will lead to greater opportunities.

Does that make sense?

Once we discover our identity, then our purpose will begin to come clear.

Purpose is in each one of us; we all exist for a reason. All of us has gifts and talents inside of us just waiting to come out. It's our gifts and talents that begin to define us as they are discovered. As we express our gifts and talents, we become aware of who we are and what direction we are to take with our life.

It's like seeds inside of us, the same way there are seeds inside a fruit. If we cut open a piece of fruit, we will find a seed in the core. When the seed is taken out and put in the proper environment, it will grow and become a tree, and it will produce even more fruit. It's the same with our lives. When we are placed in proper environments, and we live out our core values, we will begin to see our purpose, and it will begin to come to life.

I'm often asked by people how to discover what their purpose is. Many people just don't know what they are supposed to do; they don't know what their gift or purpose is. What can you do better than anyone else, or what do you like to do? Is it making things, fixing things, baking, cooking, helping people, solving problems? Whatever it is you like to do and are passionate about, that's the thing you are supposed to do; that's your gift or purpose.

Next, what can you do to improve yourself in that area? If you are a good baker, for example, look at ways you can grow your talent. Take classes, experiment, just start to improve your gift.

Then, ask yourself how you can sell what you improve. Find ways that you can begin to make money, or more money, with the talent you have. This is how you begin to define your purpose.

While you are doing this, you may need to work with, or for, someone, but find ways to refine your gift and make enough money that you can begin to support yourself.

Once we know our values, and discover our purpose, then we can begin to define success. And that's what I want to concentrate on right now.

I believe that God, The Creator, The Universe however you want to say it, longs for us to have success. God wants us to be successful, and the world needs us to bring our gifts to life. Everyone around you is depending on you to bring your gifts forward and to be successful. So, it's not only good for you to succeed, it is good for those around you to succeed. As you become your best, others around you become their best as well.

I want to share 10 success principles that I believe are foundational. These 10 success principles are clear and concise, and will help take you from A to Z in a simple and practical way.

#1 Structures

For any building to be completed successfully and stand the test of time, it must have a good solid structure.

When a big high-rise being built, they first dig a big foundation or footing before they construct the building. This is to give the structure a good solid base on which to stand. Every building must have a sub-structure or foundation. Without a solid base, the structure would be at the mercy of all the elements of weather, and it would collapse. The sheer weight of the building would be too much without a solid foundation.

In order to have success, you must have structure. After the solid base goes in for a building, you will see them start to form the shape of the building, using structural steel. The structural steel is the outline; it's the formation or frame work of the building. It's what gives the building integrity. And it's the same in our lives.

We need to have a good foundation (values) on which to build. We need to know what we are building and why (purpose). We need to know what we are building it for (success).

The foundation in our lives is what we believe in and what we stand for—our values. As the wisdom literature teaches, we all must have a solid foundation to build on. It holds true for buildings and our lives. The structure of our lives is the outlying framework—who we are and what we do. The product that our business is going to produce is part of our structure—how we conduct our business, and how we put the various components of our business and our lives together. It's the honesty, integrity, faithfulness, quality, etc. This is the structure. Without the structure, we cannot build anything that will last.

As a kid, did you ever build a house with playing cards? You would stand the cards on their edge, and lean them into each other, and then begin to build a house by stacking them on top of one another. It works for a while, until you get to a certain point where the weight starts to make it shaky. Because there is no structure, it begins to show in the stability of the card building. And it's the same with anything that we build.

Try to imagine taking the plywood and the drywall that goes into building a house, and stacking it up the same way as the cards. How far would you get with the building? You know it wouldn't be very successful without structure.

Without the structure of the foundation, the subfloors, and the walls, nothing would stand the test of time. The building wouldn't even get finished. It's the same with success in our lives and businesses. There needs to be a solid sub-structure and structure in order to complete the project.

Take the time necessary to plan your business, and take time to see what substructures are needed to go in place. For example, what is the purpose of your company or business? What are your values? What will it look like when completed?

All these things and more must be taken into account when you're building the structure.

#2 Systems

Next, you need to have systems in place. If we were to build a 40-story building, and didn't have any systems to go from one level to the next, where do you think everybody would be? Everybody would be meeting in the lobby. Nobody would be able to experience the view from the 40th floor.

Without a system to take us from one level to the next, we would all have to live on the first floor. It's the same in our lives and in business.

We need to have systems in place to help grow our businesses, day by day and week by week. We need to think of the training and the development that needs to happen, to help us grow the company. The same thing holds for us personally. We need to look at ways that we can continue to grow and develop. We need to consider how to evolve as a person. What kind of training and self-development do you need to take? What training is necessary for you to be number one in your field of choice? What do you need to do to become more productive?

Part of the systems that need to be created in business and in life will help keep order. They will help us maintain routine and flow in everything that we do. We need to arrange our time and energy in order to be more productive. Regardless of whether we have one employee or 1000 employees, systems are necessary. In fact, any project that we take on has to have a system.

Take buying a piece of unassembled furniture, for example. It comes with all the parts and components and fasteners needed to complete the piece of furniture. It also comes with a set of instructions, and these instructions give us the system needed to put the object together.

Give careful consideration to the systems you need to grow your business, your career, even relationships. Your success depends on systems to grow and evolve.

#3 Strategies

Strategies are the map that we create to help grow our business and our lives. Part of the strategy is to create goals. Do this by taking stock of what we want to do and what we want to accomplish, and begin to reverse engineer the process.

Reverse engineering is looking at the future goal, the outcome, that we want to achieve, reversing the steps that are necessary to achieve this goal, and then starting to put action steps to these goals in order to get there.

It's necessary to prioritize the goals by importance, and to always focus on the big goals. Don't allow yourself to be distracted and work on lesser goals. Always complete the big goals, and work down the list.

Brian Tracy calls them ABC goals.

A- The big goals that are your big ticket, money-producing goals. These are the things that are the most challenging but will shift you toward the big prize. Things like meeting with clients to sign deals, finalizing a plan to move a big project forward, developing programs, etc. The bigger things that you do that make you the money.

B- The less important goals. These are important tasks but are usually things that can be delegated to somebody else in order to free up your valuable time. They may be things like working on copy for sales, designing things, or fixing or repairing something. You can do them, but they could easily be handled by someone that is paid less than you or is more skilled at it.

C- The small things, like emails, Facebook, etc. These are things that don't make you money, and it doesn't really matter if you get them done right away. If you don't get on social media for a day or two, the company won't stop; yet we often lose valuable time responding and tweeting, and we lose sight of the important details needed to get the million-dollar idea launched.

With each goal, you would line up action steps to help you achieve those goals. Part of the process when coming up with strategies is to think about what you really want to achieve, and how you are going to do that. Every goal must have action steps that move you toward completing that goal. These are the small action steps that break down the big goal. It's like cutting it up into bite-size pieces.

It's like eating a big meal, the goal is to clean up the plate, and the action steps are cutting up your food, then taking one bite at a time.

Discovering strategies will undoubtedly involve masterminding.

Masterminding is key to personal and business success. Everyone needs to join a group with likeminded people so that they can gather and begin to share ideas with each other. They can share thoughts and ideas on how you can achieve the goal or build the business you want. When you gather in a mastermind, people will look at your situation in a different light and from a different angle. When they add a new piece, somebody else will add something too, and so on and so on.

This will be life-changing for you and your approach to your life or business.

Napoleon Hill, in *Think and Grow Rich*, explains that this is the only way to increase our thought processes. We all have a limited view and mental capacity to solve things. However, when we are supported in a mastermind, the thinking potential is increased 10-fold, or more, by inviting others to look at things with you.

You increase your power of thinking through other intelligent people.

Ask yourself: What is the purpose of my business? What do I want to achieve in life? As you begin to ask yourself these questions, you will begin to formulate the goals and action steps to achieve them.

#4 Speech

With each new level that we grow in, we need to adjust and refine our speech.

Now, this may seem strange or a little silly, but let me explain.

When we first start doing something that's new, the terms and language are foreign and awkward to us, so we use a language that is simple and basic, similar to when we were young.

When we were little, we may have called a blanket a *blankie*, or we may have called a bottle a *baba*. And that language was fine when we were children, because we were just learning. But could you imagine using that same language at 30 or 60 years of age? Our language needs to adjust and mature as our success grows.

When you started at a particular company, you may have spoken a particular way. The people in the new company may have used inclusive language, meaning language that only those inside the immediate circle would understand. Every circle of influence will often have its own language. They're the words that we use that only those inside our circle would clearly understand, kind of like a private joke among friends.

When people become very comfortable in their conversation, sometimes they will abbreviate words so that they don't have to say the whole thing. They do this because they know the other people in that circle will understand what they mean. However, it's foreign to outsiders, and they need to take time to understand it.

You may have used a lot of slang or curse words. These words are often used because the person using them doesn't have a very big vocabulary. It becomes convenient to use foul words, over and over, rather than search for new, more accurate ones.

As you grow and mature as a leader or business owner, you will need to expand your language so that everyone that you speak with understands you. That means not using abbreviated terms when you write emails, like LOL or NP (laugh out loud and no problem), or using foul or slang words. The more open and inclusive you are with your communication skills, the more successful you will be. As you move up in business, so should your language.

Your speech or language should reflect your attitude, personality, and position; it demonstrates your maturity. I've heard people use very colorful language when they talk in professional settings, and they just don't look the type to use that kind of language, nor is it fitting. Always remember to use language that's reflective of who you are as a person and as a professional.

One afternoon, while working on something on my computer, I remember struggling to get a program to install and update. I worked at this for some time, and it wasn't cooperating. It was one of those tasks that I had done several times before, but for some reason, it just wasn't working.

On the best of days, computers can test anybody; and on this particular day, I lost my temper. I mean, I just blew a gasket while working on my computer.

I recall sitting back in my chair, after the explosion, and

saying, "What on earth just happened, and where did that come from?" I became painfully aware that at that moment, my language didn't reflect who I was as a person; nor did it reflect the character, attitude or the integrity of the man I am.

I remember the words I said, and the way I responded was not indicative of who I want to reflect. That day, I committed to myself that I would not allow my language, or attitude, to get the best of me.

Your speech is important.

People around may be paying closer attention to you than you think. Keep in mind that once words are spoken, they can't be taken back. A word spoken out of frustration or rage can have damaging effects. It could be harmful to a personal relationship, or even that of a client or co-worker. You can apologize, and you can be forgiven, but the sting of that moment may live on for a while.

The tendency, for some, is to believe that if nobody is around to witness what's going on, then it's okay. Part of the journey to becoming a person of integrity is to be the same person in public as you are in private. Ultimately, there is no place to drop your guard and act as a lesser person. Integrity doesn't take holidays. Determine to be the same person, even when nobody's watching.

Guard your tongue, and be mindful of your speech.

#5 Sacrifice

A person that has high values, and that wants to be successful in business and in life, will need to make sacrifice along the way.

It will cost you greatly to be successful, on more levels than you can imagine. Not only are there financial sacrifices that you need to endure along the pathway, there will also be emotional and physical sacrifices as well.

There may come a time where you need to put that new car off for one more year. Or you may need to put that trip off for a longer period of time. You will experience times when you can't join in on some social events because you need to finish a proposal or write that blog.

Times will come when you will need to put something off so that, in the long term, you will gain more.

There will be times where you will need to delay gratification. That means putting off something enjoyable for a longer period of time, in order to achieve success. If you want to have all the benefits of success, without the work, you will be disappointed.

Psychologists conducted a study on a group of grade-one students. The students were all told that they could each have a marshmallow. You can imagine how excited they were.

Then they were told that the teachers were going to leave the room, and that if they would wait for fifteen minutes and not eat their marshmallow, when the teachers returned, they could have a second marshmallow. They could have two marshmallows if they would delay eating the marshmallow in front on them for fifteen minutes. The looks on their faces were priceless.

The children agonized, and some came up with creative ideas so that they couldn't see the treat sitting right in front of their face. They covered their faces, or folded paper over top of the marshmallow, and some turned around in their seats.

Needless to say, only a few students actually waited to get the second treat. For most of them, the one that they could have immediately, was good enough.

Many of us act the same way. It is much easier to just take

what we can now, and not wait for better returns in the future. It takes discipline to resist the easy and the available. When a group of friends asks you to join them for dinner and to enjoy an evening, it's tempting to go and enjoy, and to forget what needs to be done.

Let me interject something here, if I may. We all need to have breaks and to enjoy life. It makes no sense to be so isolated that we don't have any fun. I mean, after all, life is a journey, not just a destination. It's important that we schedule those times in. What I'm talking about here is making a plan and being disciplined enough to put off the easy to make the dream happen.

Use your weekly schedule, and make space for such moments, especially when it comes to family, and your spouse or partner. Schedule quality time with those that are important to you. It doesn't have to be big chunks of time, but it does need to be quality time in order to build strong moments.

For me, I like to break things down into smaller portions. For example, I like a nice craft beer or a nice glass of wine sometimes with a meal. If I know I have a busy week, with lots of meetings and lots of goals to achieve, I will set a night through the week, or at the end of the week, where I will treat myself to a glass of wine or something with a meal. But this only happens if I achieve a certain goal.

With my weekly schedule, I carve out time throughout the week for me and for the events that are important. For example, the first two hours in the morning are for me. I exercise, read, pray, have a good breakfast, and get set for the day. If I'm not travelling and don't need to be out for meetings, my wife and I schedule two hours each night for dinner and to spend time together.

Mr. Brian Tracy uses the example of the cookies. He teaches

people to have a tray of cookies, broken into little pieces, sitting beside them on their desk. Each time they reach a level of 10 or 20 calls, they reward themselves with a piece of cookie (You can substitute cookies for anything that works for your diet.).

I suggest that you have little rewards for achievements you make through the week, and a bigger reward when you've accomplished a big goal, say at the end of the month. This not only gives you something to look forward to, but it also gives you something that drives you forward to accomplish your goal.

It takes discipline to maintain this course for success. Remember, if you succeed, you will not only have the amazing feeling of success; there just might be a second marshmallow in it for your effort.

You will also need to sacrifice greatly in order to keep from compromising your values. If, for example, one of your values is to be truthful in every situation, then you need to be mindful of the situations that you open yourself up to.

Do not put yourself in a position where you are tempted to compromise your honesty. In the same way that an alcoholic must be aware of their environment all the time, you don't want to put yourself at risk and find yourself in a place where you will be tempted to compromise.

You and I need to do the same thing. In order to stay in a good position and to uphold our values, we need to sacrifice and keep ourselves out of environments and out of positions that may cause us to fail.

Be mindful of your surroundings.

Always be prepared for any situation. If you are meeting with a client, make sure that you are prepared to give all the answers and data you may be required to give. One of the things that happens is if we are unprepared to answer something, we just begin to make stuff up. We start reaching and grasping, and before long, we may find our back to the wall, and we start offering things we can't deliver, or we overpromise and then regret the deal. We can find ourselves in a place where we may stretch the truth.

Instead of telling stories and making stuff up, be prepared and decide ahead of time that if you don't know something, you will tell people you will get back to them.

That's honesty and walking in integrity.

#6 Sustain

The word, *sustain*, means to keep something from falling or collapsing.

We have looked at the importance creating structures and systems. As well, we looked at the importance of creating strategies to start moving toward our goals. Now we need to sustain the momentum to achieve success.

We can't stop prematurely. We need to be constantly moving toward reaching our goal of success. We need to keep the momentum going; we need to sustain our mobility and movement toward our goal, while being ever mindful of our surroundings, and even more mindful of looking after ourselves.

Getting caught up in our success goals, we can forget to look after ourselves. The busier we become, the more challenging it can be to stay focused on our health. I find it easier to grab something on the run than to make something myself. When I get tired, it's tempting to go to the take-out window at any restaurant, and place an order.

Have you ever found that? Tired, busy, and working hard can sometimes be the formula for fast food, which equals declining health and energy because eating fast food you're just filling your stomach not fueling your body.

The easiest way to keep ourselves sustained is to keep ourselves healthy and balanced. Make sure you're getting proper rest. Make sure you are eating and drinking properly, especially when you get busy.

Don't become so focused that you lose sight of what's really important. Remember, if you don't have good health, you don't have anything. Your health is valuable for success. Continue to put healthy choices in front of you.

When we start to get overtired or overworked, it's easier to start losing that momentum. Refer back to the balance chapter often, to get even more direction and encouragement there. And have an accountability partner or group, someplace where you can share how you are doing, where you may be struggling and where you know people will encourage you to get back on track.

Over the years, I have made over fifteen trips to Central America to do short-term mission work. I have been involved with several self-sustaining projects there. I would meet with a group, and we would identify some good projects and then raise the capital to get the project going.

Part of the sustainability we were looking for were projects that, once they were kick-started, would continue to move forward. All they needed was initial capital to buy some resources or materials, and then they could begin to generate enough income to support themselves. Once going, they didn't need any other help from the outside. The only time it would fail is if the momentum didn't keep going within the company or the project.

It was important to install systems and structures to assist the momentum.

It's the same with you and with me. Once we get the structure and systems in place, we need to keep the sustainability moving forward. Keep that momentum moving forward. Do everything in your power to keep your health and your strength, and move toward success.

Ask yourself: What system do I need to put in place to keep things feeding themselves? Constantly think of things you can implement in your life so that it keeps feeding itself.

What systems can you put in place in your business, workplace, or career to keep things feeding itself?

Sustainability is key. Make the effort to identify ways to keep things feeding themselves.

The less energy and time you have to throw at something, the more energy you have to build other things.

#7 Seize

Carpe Diem—seize the day!

Every day that you are able to get up and start moving, is a good day. As the old expression goes, any day on the green side of the grass is a good day. With every day, you need to seize the opportunities.

Seize the day and every opportunity that comes toward you. Never take for granted a new day, and never put off until tomorrow what you can do today. There's a proverb that teaches this: A little rest and a little folding of the hands, and poverty comes in like a thief.

By making the most of each day, we keep poverty at bay. Making the most of each day, and the most of every opportunity, is vital for our success, because we never know how many days we're going to have, and we never know exactly what a day is going to bring. So, when you get up, start moving forward in order to continually and systematically work your plan toward your success.

Take advantage of any opportunity when it comes along, because sometimes when an opportunity presents itself, it may never present itself a second time. It may be a once-in-a-lifetime opportunity. Therefore, seize the moment and seize the day. Never put off what you can do at a given moment, to do it at a later time.

Think less and just do!

During one summer vacation, my wife and I were driving through the eastern provinces of my country, on our motorcycle. And as is often the case, when we were driving, we would take opportunities to stop at unique shops or restaurants.

I remember one time driving along, and we saw a sign for a particular store that we thought would be interesting to check out. However, because we wanted to reach a certain point by the end of the day, we decided to make a mental note of the place so that we could stop in and explore on our way back. We both figured it would be easy since we were coming back the exact same route. After all, how hard would it be to look for that store?

Guess what happened?

On our return, we couldn't find it. We drove back and forth around the area where we knew that sign was, but we couldn't find it anywhere. Now, it wasn't life or death for us to go and see this store. The point is that had we stopped when we saw it, we may have enjoyed that moment. It may have been a great memory, or there may have been some great things for us to explore or learn about. But now we will never know, because that moment had passed.

I'm sure that as you're reading these words, you're thinking of times in your life where you wished you would have seized an opportunity. Instead, you allowed other things to take priority, and you didn't do it. It's more the regret or the disappointment that you didn't do it than anything else. The one major factor that keeps most of us from stopping and enjoying more, is time. We never think that we have enough time, or we think we can do it some other time, so we don't take advantage of opportunities.

There are going to be critical opportunities that present themselves, and if we don't take the opportunities when presented at that given moment, they will be lost forever.

You see, the same way we want to keep momentum going in our business, momentum is going in the whole world—the whole universe. Everything is moving forward. So, for us to backtrack to try to find something, it could be twice as hard to find it, because everything else is moving forward at the same time we're trying to backtrack.

Does that make sense?

Things in the world are moving forward, and when we try to backtrack to try to find things or to take advantage of an opportunity that presented itself, it is still moving forward, and we may never see it or catch up to it.

Let's say that somebody speaks to us and invites us to partner up with them on a business deal. It's a good opportunity, but you are unsure if you want to join them. You've been thinking about doing something, but you're not sure. They try to convince you, but you say you'll consider it and get back to them, then go on your way.

You both go forward. Now you go through your day and start thinking that it would be a good idea, so you begin to backtrack to find them, call them, and discuss the terms again. Now you've taken time out of your moving forward toward your goals, to go back to talk about this deal. In the meantime, they are still moving. They are moving toward their goal of finding a joint venture partner and selling this idea.

After a time, you connect, and find that they have made the deal—it's gone. Now you need to re-engage in what you were doing before this all started, and get back on track.

Can you see the time that is lost? Because things are moving forward, when we lose momentum and try to go back to gain something, we may kill the momentum. We also use a lot of time and energy.

The point is to always be prepared. I know that sounds like a Boy Scout motto, but it is true with everything we do. Be prepared and seize the day. Know what you want, where you are going, and what you have to invest. At any given time, be prepared to make the decisions quick, while the momentum is going with you.

It's necessary that we train ourselves to be aware of this, and take advantage of opportunities when they come to us.

#8 Stop

It's sometimes necessary to pause and stop from time to time.

It's good to stop and reflect. It's especially important to stop and reflect on our personal lives. Take time for self-examination of your heart, of your motives, and the direction you are going.

While you are stopped, take time to reflect on meetings or appointments that you had during the day, or the days prior, and ask yourself some tough questions. How did I do in that meeting? Did I respond appropriately to their comments? Did I make a good impression? Are there things that I could do differently? How were my interactions with my partner, family, or friends?

As you stop and ask yourself these questions, begin to examine ways that you could do things better or differently.

Would you agree that we could all do things better? Take time to stop and reflect, and look at ways that you could do things differently. Begin to take notes, and journal ways that you could do things differently. Write out different examples of how you could say things when you go into meetings with clients. If you know you're going to be meeting with somebody that is particularly challenging for you, begin to rehearse ways that you can be polite and courteous.

Look at your family and personal life. Sometimes we can leave home in the morning in no uncertain terms. You know; you woke up late, or everyone was running behind, making it extra challenging to get out the door on time. Things get said, and tempers fly, and things may have been less than ideal. Examine the events, and ask yourself: Are there ways I can handle my personal relationships differently?

These are just a few of the things that you can do when you stop to reflect. Be sure to take time throughout the day and throughout your week to reflect on ways that you can do things better.

Take inventory regularly, and adjust as needed. You can also read books and articles that other people in the same situation have written, and glean some advice or tips. That's the great thing about the time we live in; we can ask any question online and get endless advice or ideas.

When we stop and reflect, it's amazing what we can learn about ourselves. By constantly applying new techniques, we will be moving forward to being the person we were created to be.

Plus, we are moving that much closer to our success goals.

#9 Start

The next step is to start!

Once you've taken the time to stop and reflect on things that you could do differently, the next natural step is to start.

Start implementing those things that you journaled in your book. Start doing the things that you played out in your mind. Make it your intention to begin to start doing things differently. If you get in a conversation or a similar situation that you've already worked through, make the choice to start approaching it differently.

Don't try to implement every trick and every new tactic at once. Gradually work things into your conversations. Introduce new ideas at home and work. You will begin to see progress as you go. Introduce something, and then once you've adjusted to that one idea, add something else, and so on.

If you make a mistake and go back into the old routine, as so often is the case, stop yourself and start again. You don't need to beat yourself up over this. Simply stop, remember what you were going to do, and start again.

But keep the momentum moving forward. Keep the traction moving in the direction that you want to go. Remember, control everything that goes into your mind and that comes out of your mouth.

Once you've loaded the words into your mouth, it's very difficult to stop. Realize that you have the control of what goes into your mind and what comes out of your mouth. As the old expression goes, *"Garbage in, garbage out."*

You control what goes into your mind. If it's crap, then crap is likely to come out of your mouth. The more valuable and useful the data is that you put in your mind, and the more you adjust your thinking and approach, the more likely that great stuff will come out of your mouth.

What we speak is often a reflection of what's in the heart.

Start each day with gratitude. Start each day with praying

and meditating. This is the best way to start your day. Spending time when you first get up will set the stage for the rest of your day. It's important to get our minds right for the day.

It's equally as important to continue, even through the day, to take a few moments from time to time, and get your heart and mind right again. The business of the day can throw us off track sometimes.

When you think about each day, remember that it is a connection to the next day. One day runs into the next day. What you're really doing is setting yourself up for the week. Because time runs so closely and continuously, it becomes even more critical to examine our heart each day. With practice, this will set us up for the days and weeks to come.

Speaking of the week, don't forget to start writing out your goal sheet. At the beginning of every week, start scheduling your time (reach out to me at jimhetherington.com and I'll send you the form I use). From Monday to Sunday, begin blocking out the time that you need for you, your family, for your rest, for your work, to work on goals and action steps, etc. Begin each week with the discipline of writing out your goals for the week.

You'll be amazed at how much more you can achieve.

#10 Smile

Remember to smile!
This is the last success word that I want to leave you with.
Do you know how powerful a smile is? Through just smiling, you can change your whole countenance. By just smiling, you can change your mood and disposition, because you can't operate in a negative and positive emotion at the same time.

It's true.

You cannot carry a negative and positive emotion at the same time. Whenever you feel miserable or down, try smiling. The simple act of smiling will begin to release endorphins in your brain. Just a simple smile begins to release the happy drug, all through your body. These endorphins will begin to instantly make you feel better. This natural happy drug, when released, begins to charge you, and it will change your attitude instantly.

There is conflict about whether it takes more or less muscles to smile or frown. Some studies say it takes more to smile and others say it takes more to frown. Regardless if it takes more or less it does take more energy emotionally, mentally, and physically to keep frowning and to stay miserable. The heaviness that comes over us when we are down is weighing. Why would anyone want to stay miserable, and consume that much energy, when there is no value?

It's also been said that it will help reduce wrinkles; but that's in dispute medically as well :-) Smiling just feels better!

There was a television show that I watched some time ago, called *That 70s Show*. In the show, the mother, Kitty Forman, would laugh at the most inappropriate times. Everyone, including the audience, thought it was so peculiar. In one episode, her son asked why she laughed when everybody was angry, or when somebody was getting upset. She explained that if she smiled or laughed when she felt heavy or sad, then she would feel better. This is the science behind this discovery I'm sharing.

A simple smile will change your entire countenance.

This will lift the weight off you, and begin to lighten up the mood. It will keep you from becoming miserable and staying in a foul mood. I thought it was just entertaining and funny the way Kitty Forman cackled when she laughed. But it turned out that there was an amazing science behind what she was doing.

Sometimes when I get up in the morning, when I'm extra tired, I will smile as I'm getting out of bed. It's amazing how I can go from being dead tired to feeling a little energy boost, just by smiling.

Smile often.

I trust this helps you understand the process of success a little better. By taking these success principles and applying them to your life, you will begin to grow toward your goals, and achieve more than you could ever achieve before. Spending time learning, reading, and developing yourself will take you toward the goals that you have designed.

Remember that you need to clearly define what success is, and then begin the process of setting up the structures and systems that you need to achieve those goals. Once you know what your goals are, add action steps to help you accomplish these goals. It's the action steps that will get things done more quickly.

One of the greatest things you can do daily is to take inventory of your past actions and events. Deal with things in your past so that you can move forward more freely. Unforgiveness, pain, and resentment can slow you down and keep you from the success you desire and deserve.

I wish you the greatest success in all you do, whatever that looks like for you.

What steps are you going to take now as a result of reading this material? How are you going to begin to implement these new tools?

If you need further assistance in defining success, writing out success goals, or creating action steps, I'm here to help.

Let me offer a no-obligation consultation. If there are particular points that you are struggling with, it may only take a

simple email or a one-time call to get you over that hurdle. If it's more, we can discuss what that looks like for you.
The goal is your success.
Don't struggle—reach out. I can be reached at jim@jimhetherington.com.
To your great success!

Thoughts

Thoughts

Part 8

What Now?

"Start with the end in mind and you'll discover where to start."
— Jim Hetherington

Red Lights are Good

There are three types of people when it comes to learning.

If you're an average person, you may not read or study a whole lot. Studies have shown that the average person only reads 2-4 books per year after they have finished going to school. Once classes are done and the diploma is earned, people stop reading.

The next category would be above average. These people will read newspapers, magazines, and books, but more for pleasure. They follow things only to stay current, and they read 4-8 books per year.

The third category is where I'm believing you are. The people in this category are life learners, and they study to excel. They read 8-50 books per year. They read to grow and develop themselves, and to become their best.

The problem in this category is that sometimes they take so many courses that they don't know what to do with the information they have learned. They study and study, and learn and learn, but they do little with the material they take in. They just shovel it into their mind, and then put the books and study material on the shelf. I met Jack Canfield, and through our conversation, he called it, "shelf-esteem." We feel good that we took yet another course and read another book, but the knowledge ends up on our shelf rather than in our hearts.

So, really, what do we do?

I have a thought. Most of us get frustrated with traffic lights. I mean, we all want to fly through our day and never get stopped. The problem is that as we plow through our day, we miss opportunities to stop, reflect, and grow.

Right now, you may be heading down a road, and you're uncertain how to really succeed. Or you're uncertain if you are heading down the right path. It could also be that you have circumstances coming at you, and you don't know what to do. You want to keep going, but is it the right thing to do? I have a suggestion.

Think about this:

Many times, in life, we run into situations that we are not sure how to deal with. We may formulate a plan as we go, with the hopes that things will work out. It is like driving along and all the traffic lights are green, and then you come up and one turns yellow. Then we have a decision to make. Are we going to speed up and try to race through it, or are we going to lock-on the brakes? Or are we going to just casually slow down and come to a stop.

It's the same in our personal lives, our work lives, and our spiritual lives. We have that same approach when we come up to a situation that is unexpected or that we are not sure of. We treat it like that yellow light: We could rush through without thinking about the consequences; we could jam on the brakes and stop everything because we can't handle it; or we could slow down and take the time to access the situation.

Yellow lights are important in our lives. If we are in a situation, let's say in a business meeting that didn't go that well, the yellow light could be where we slow down and consider what we said, and think about how we could have changed what we said. We can evaluate the delivery, or evaluate what we spoke. We can rethink how we approached the meeting or situation.

The problem is that sometimes when we get into those situations, we try to push our way through, like speeding up to get through the yellow light before it changes. We don't want to stop. We don't want to take the time to evaluate what happened, or to realize that maybe we were wrong, and that maybe there are things we need to change.

The yellow light is the time to slow down and think about that meeting, proposal, or relationship, and how we interacted with that person. We can look at ways that we can adjust our thinking, and consider how we could have done things differently—look at the whole thing and be honest with ourselves.

The yellow stands for "yell out." We could yell out or speak out the frustration or tension we feel, and then be open to adjust our thinking and our mindsets.

The red light stands for "redo our thinking." We reset our mindset and re-shift ourselves to decide how we are going to approach the situation if we get into that situation again.

Red lights are a great time to reposition our hearts, to redirect our attitude. Red lights aren't always an inconvenience; they are for our good. By taking the time to really look at our heart and attitude, we can then move forward in a more positive manner.

My friend and mentor, Raymond Aaron, was telling of a time when he was driving in traffic with someone and they got caught up in traffic. It was stop and go the entire time and consequently they were late for their engagement. When they arrived, the person that was with him complained about how awful the drive was. Raymond on the other hand stated how he enjoyed the ride. Why? Because he was thankful to be in an air-conditioned, comfortable car where he could enjoy some music and reflect on things that had gone on in his day.

Most of us have been frustrated with something or someone in the past—I mean, so frustrated that you could just spit, and steam is coming out of your nostrils because you are so frustrated. Rather than giving in, you persistently press on, trying to win the argument or get your point across. You're not giving in, and neither are they.

You keep at the task with all the determination in the world, trying to overcome the obstacle. Finally, after a trying time, you stop and take a break. You get some fresh air, take a little walk, count to ten, and take deep breaths. Then, to your amazement, you go back to the situation and it's like a cloud has lifted. All of a sudden, you're communicating, and it is actually working. You try the task again, and all the parts fit and work as planned.

It's a miracle! No.

That's the result of slowing down (yellow light) and then stopping (red light) and seeing things in a new light.

Which leads us to the next step: the green light.

The green light is when you get going and decide that you are going to use that new mindset; you are going to move forward and do things differently. This is where you apply what you have learned during the yellow and red lights.

It's the same in the relationships in your life. You can ignore what is going on, or you can reflect and allow the relationship to become stronger.

What Are You Waiting for?

Let me give you a practical example.

How many times has this situation happened? It's 7:00 in the morning, you got up late, you are rushing to get everybody ready to go off to school or work, and there are tensions and frustrations, and everyone is getting under each other's feet. You part ways, and everyone, including you, is in a sour mood. By the time you get to work, you are disheartened and ready to throw in the towel; you'd rather go back home to bed. You have to go through the day thinking about it, going over in your mind what went wrong, how it went wrong, and the awful things that were said.

The yellow light could be where you pause and say to yourself, "How can I take a different approach to the way I spoke to my spouse or to my children, or to my significant other? How can I realign myself and handle the situation in a different way?"

The red light is realizing that you can't control that other person. You can't always control your work scenario or your home scenario, but you can control yourself and the way that you react. I can control the way I speak out. I control my attitude. I don't have to allow my children or spouse to change my attitude. I can take responsibility for that, and keep it in check.

The green light is to go and work on implementing the ideas you came up with, starting with taking full responsibility and recognizing that only you can control you.

Sometimes in your spiritual life, you can get frustrated with the Universe, with the world, and with God, because you don't think you're receiving all you should, or you think that you aren't getting what you desire.

That yellow light would be recognizing that something is not right inside you or around you, because you feel like you are being ripped off or not getting the answers that you want. Many times, those emotions are deep down, and you don't see them; you only feel the effects of them.

The red light is to sit and realign yourself with your core values and your core beliefs, and see that God and the Universe can be trusted, and that it's your beliefs that need to be strengthened. As you ask for guidance, it will come—in time. This is where faith comes in. You put action to your mindset and see it become reality.

One of the dangers of racing through the yellow light, and ignoring that warning, is that by the time you get through the intersection, that light could be red. Now you are not going through a caution warning; you are going through a red light, and there could be consequences.

From the driving side of things, you know what that is. If there is a police officer nearby, they could be hot on your tail, pulling you over and giving you a traffic violation. That could mean points, or a fine—it could be a lot of things. If you require that license for business, for travelling, and for making your income, you can only lose so many points, and then you are going to start getting into trouble.

It's the same in life. If you ignore these caution signs—the yellow lights—and keep pressing through them, you are going to have to face the consequences.

The consequences in your business life could be continuing to not make sales. If you are unwilling to adjust your attitude or approach, then the consequence is that you may never get customers and have the success you want.

Make a Plan

In relationships, if you keep plowing through, thinking that there is nothing wrong, that the yellow light is for somebody else, then the consequence is that you are going to have a very unhappy, unfulfilled relationship. The frustrating and confrontational situations may never go away or get resolved.

If you think that everybody else is the problem, then you are never going to grow, or have a healthy/happy relationship. We need to take time, slow down, and then stop completely, and re-evaluate our approach to relationships before proceeding with a new attitude.

If a problem or situation arises, slow down and consider it (yellow light), stop and consider what you can do differently (red light), and then take action on the things you considered (green light).

It's easy to get into the habit of just doing your job or going through your routines. If you don't adjust, the danger is that you can become stunted, and then you won't grow and mature as a person.

Science has shown that by the time you are 35 years of age, 90 percent of your thinking is just habitual. If you don't interrupt the routine and build new habits, you will begin to lose your creativeness. If you don't re-evaluate and replace old habits, and you don't create new habits, there is a danger of becoming the same person all the way through into the later stages in life.

My encouragement to you? You need to step back and evaluate your life—daily, weekly, monthly, and yearly. You can only grow when you see what you must change. It's nobody else's responsibility to change to what you want. You need to become more. You need to evaluate yourself.

Those yellow lights are the perfect time to pause and prepare to stop at the red lights, and to take a reality check. What areas of your life need adjustment? What areas can you improve in?

Have you ever watched drivers going down the highway and cutting in and out, running lights and so on? They seldom get that much further ahead. Slow down and enjoy the ride. Take time and do an inventory check.

Remember that what you do affects everyone else. By changing yourself for the better, not only will others see the change, but it will encourage them to do the same.

Want to become a world changer? Start in your circle of influence. Start with your family and your close relationships.

Don't look at red lights as an inconvenience anymore. If you need to stop at one, STOP! Take the time to be grateful. Take the time to think about things in your life that you could change. Think of past encounters or meetings, and think about how you might handle them differently next time. Don't rush through; stop and reflect. Practice being grateful.

You may feel overwhelmed right now, or at the edge of burnout. When you hit those times in life, it feels like life is impossible and that nothing will ever change take time to re-evaluate, and move forward.

When things are at their worst, that is when you need to heed the yellow light and slow down and evaluate. If you keep speeding through life, refusing to stop, circumstances will eventually catch up with you. The consequences of barreling through life may be dire.

Make the choice now to slow down or stop. Then reflect, reset, and go.

Next Steps for You!

Allow me to share a few more tips from the wisdom of T.D. Jakes that will help you in any area of life. They can be applied to any relationship, career change or new venture you take on, and to any goal or habit you want to achieve.

Remember anything you want to change on the outside needs to be changed on the inside as well.

1 – Know what you want. We've talked about setting goals, looking to the future, and going for it. Now you really need to know what you want. When you know what you want, nothing will stop you. Make your plan and work on it diligently.

2 – Adjust your attitude. Don't let the things that happened in your past affect what you look like moving forward. Sometimes when life gets tough, we can show that on our face. We can look down or frightened. Don't. Get rid of those old expressions—smile, lift yourself up, and look like you're ready for a new thing. Don't get defeated, get motivated.

3 – Change your expressions. Remember that your attitude affects where you're going. Have the attitude of a winner, of one who is confident of where they are going. Look at the world with new eyes. Make your focus where you are going and not the obstacles or distractions in the way.

4 – Dress for the part. Once you act the part and adjust your attitude for the part, start to dress the part. If it's the corner office you're going for, then dress the part of the corner office. You need to be dressed and ready to take the position or the place you want to fill. Always be prepared for success.

5 – It may feel unnatural. You may find that staying where

you were feels awkward, and being in the new area that you want to be in feels strange, but get used to it. It may feel uncomfortable at first, but you'll get used to the surroundings, the people, and the new routines. We all need to go through growth and change to be successful, so don't let the new surroundings and the new routines hold you back.

My council to you is to have a mentor, coach, or friend that can walk you through these steps. As you succeed, you need to be wise as to how to handle yourself appropriately. Part of true success is being gracious. Nobody likes a loud know-it-all that shoots their mouth off. Look the part, be the part, and speak the part in good time.

If you find it a challenge to implement any of the tools and ideas that I've shared, I would love to help you. I'd be delighted to come alongside you and give you more instruction to get started, and to continue even further as you head down the road to greater success. You won't be able to apply everything you learn straight away. It all takes time. In fact, it can take 100-300 days to establish new habits and continue to refine yourself for success. That's why it is key to have a coach with you along the way. I can remind you of the areas that may trip you up, as well as potential hurdles, and create a plan with you for massive success.

If you want to know more about me, or if you would like some other resources, go to www.jimhetherington.com, and check out the resources I have available. They will change your focus in your relationships, and make them better than ever.

You can also book a complimentary session by emailing me at jim@jimhetherington.com. Let's connect and see how I can guide you to a fulfilled life, with awesome relationships with your family, friends, and co-workers, and most importantly, YOU.

Learn to become a master at identifying key areas in your

life that you need to redefine. Remember to take a hard look in the mirror, and examine your heart often. Don't allow the lies of love to derail you and convince you of anything less than the best that love has for you.

Keep the laws of love close.

Your success is ready to be designed and filled. You can and will make a difference. Keep on course, keep trusted people in your circle, and keep good council with a coach or mentor.

I leave you with these final thoughts. Ask yourself: What will I do now? What areas can I improve on? How will I benefit relationally, physically, financially and spiritually from what I improve on?

Remember, I'm here for you.

To your greater success,
Jim

Thoughts

Thoughts

About the Author

Jim Hetherington is the Relationship Breakthrough Specialist. He is an international award-winning #1 bestselling author and recipient of awards like "The Influential Authority Award." Jim is also an International speaker and teacher.

Through his work as a Relationship Breakthrough Specialist, his clients become more aware of their communication, they manage their expectations of themselves and others, and take massive action steps to achieve a more balanced life.

Jim's desire is that everyone has amazing relationships in their personal, business and spiritual life. His clients describe him as genuine, thoughtful, wise; a man of integrity.

Jim has been featured on NBC, ABC, Fox and other networks.

Are you attracting the relationships you want? Do you find you are always out of time and life seems out of balance? Do you want to discover more? Schedule a complimentary session and let Jim show you how you can have more.

Jim is also available to speak at your event, deliver presentations and do workshops.

For rates and availability contact him directly at: www.jimhetherington.com, or by email jim@jimhetherington.com and at www.coachjim360.com. When you visit the website be sure to look for more articles and resources.

To order more books go to www.jimhetherington.com or www.amazon.com.

www.ingramcontent.com/pod-product-compliance
Lightning Source LLC
LaVergne TN
LVHW051557070426
835507LV00021B/2631